FORD MADOX FORD

In the same series:

    (*continued on page 158*)

MODERN LITERATURE MONOGRAPHS
GENERAL EDITOR: Lina Mainiero

FORD MADOX FORD

Sondra J. Stang

FREDERICK UNGAR PUBLISHING CO.
NEW YORK

Library of Congress Cataloging in Publication Data

Stang, Sondra J
  Ford Madox Ford.

  (Modern literature monographs)
  Bibliography: p.
  Includes index.
  1. Ford, Ford Madox, 1873-1939—Criticism and inter-
pretation.
PR6011.053Z9   828'.9'1209   77-41
ISBN 0-8044-2832-8

For Miriam and for Richard

Acknowledgments

I would like to thank Professor Arthur Mizener for permission to reprint his chronology of the events of *Parade's End*, published by The New American Library in the Signet Classic edition. I would like also to thank the editor of *Modern Language Quarterly* for permission to reprint material from my essay "A Reading of *The Good Soldier*" (December 1969).

I am very grateful to the successive directors of the Rare Book Room of Olin Library, Washington University, St. Louis—Mr. William Matheson, Mr. Roger Mortimer, Ms. Holly Hall—and the staff for putting the Ford collection at my disposal and for being extraordinarily attentive and helpful. And I thank Professor Scott Elledge and the Rare Book Department of Cornell University for help in enabling me to use unpublished Ford material.

Contents

Chronology

1873:	Ford Hermann Hueffer is born on December 17 in Merton, Surrey.
1889:	Death of father, Dr. Francis Hueffer; family moved to house of the grandfather, Ford Madox Brown.
1891:	Conversion to Roman Catholicism. His first publication, *The Brown Owl*, a fairy tale for children.
1892:	Publication of his first novel, *The Shifting of the Fire*.
1893:	Death of grandfather.
1894:	Elopement with Elsie Martindale.
1896:	Publication of *Ford Madox Brown: A Record of His Life and Work*.
1897:	Birth of daughter Christina.
1898:	Meeting with Conrad, arranged by Stephen Crane and Edward Garnett; beginning of ten-year collaboration: *The Inheritors* (1901), *Romance* (1903), *The Nature of a Crime* (1909).
1900:	Birth of daughter Katherine.
1904:	Nervous collapse; trip to Germany.
1906–08:	Publication of *The Fifth Queen* trilogy: *The Fifth Queen, Privy Seal, The Fifth Queen Crowned*.
1908–09:	Editorship of the *English Review*.

1908:   Meeting with Violet Hunt, with whom he
             lived until 1915; collaboration with her on
             The Desirable Alien (1913) and *Zeppelin
             Nights* (1915).

1910:   Residence in Germany to obtain a divorce
             from Elsie under German law.

1910–11:   Elsie's refusal to grant divorce and her libel
             suit of two newspapers referring to Violet
             Hunt as Mrs. Hueffer; Ford's bankruptcy and
             sale of all his possessions as a result of legal ex-
             penses of attempted divorce and debts of
             English Review.

1915:   Publication of *The Good Soldier*. Death of
             Ford's friend, the sculptor Gaudier-Brjeska, in
             the war and Ford's enlistment in the British
             army; active service at the front from July 1916.

1918:   Meeting with the painter Stella Bowen, a
             friend of Ezra Pound.

1919:   Change of name to Ford Madox Ford. Move to
             Sussex with Stella.

1920:   Birth of daughter Esther Julia Ford (Julie).

1921:   Award by *Poetry* magazine of $100 prize for
             his poem *A House* (the only literary prize of
             his career).

1922:   Move to France with Stella and Julie.

1924–25:   Editorship of the *transatlantic review*.

1924:   *Some Do Not . . .* ; Conrad's death; Ford's
             Joseph Conrad: A Personal Remembrance;
             affair with Jean Rhys.

1925:   *No More Parades.*

1926:   *A Man Could Stand Up—.*

1927:   Separation from Stella.

1928:   *Last Post.*

1930:   Meeting with the painter Janice Biala, with
             whom he lived until his death.

1931–36:   Publication of last novels.

1934–36:   Travels in the United States.

1936:   *Collected Poems* published by Oxford University Press.

1937:   Appointment at Olivet College, Michigan.

1939:   Death in Deauville, France on June 26, 1939.

1

~~~~~~~~~~~~~~~~~~~~~~~~~~~~~~~~~~~~

Toward an Appreciation of Ford

"The man who did the *work* for English writing was Ford Madox Hueffer (now Ford)." Ezra Pound was, in his enthusiasm, speaking of the writer known as Ford Madox Ford after he changed his surname in 1919. Pound never tired of proclaiming Ford's importance. What Ford had taught him he passed on to Yeats and Joyce and Eliot. And in a profusion of statements Pound recorded his gratitude:

I would rather talk about poetry with Ford Madox Hueffer than with any man in London.

Mr. Hueffer is the best critic in England, one might say the only critic of any importance.

The revolution of the word began so far as it affected the men who were of my age in London in 1908 with the LONE whimper of Ford Madox Hueffer.

Ford knew the answer but no one believed him. . . .

I think you shd. go find *out* what ole Fordie wuz drivin at; and eschew Mr. Eliot's affected and artyficial language.[1]

In this last statement Pound was referring to Ford's insistence on the need for a new kind of living language both in poetry and in prose. Poetry had to have the clarity and accuracy, the naturalness and hardness of prose; and prose had to be written at least (as Pound often repeated) as carefully as poetry, with as much attention to patterns of sound. Pound spoke of the "cleaning" of the word. *Le mot juste* ("just wording," Ford translated it) was the term Ford and Conrad used in their endless discussions on the art of the novel during the years of their collaboration, and their use of the French term made it plain that they looked to the nineteenth-century novel for a great deal. Flaubert, Stendhal, Maupassant, Turgenev (for Ford and Conrad, Turgenev was *French*) were not only to influence the use of language in the English novel but to redirect the nature of its construction and alter the kinds of comments the novel can make about life.

"It was Ford, and Ford almost alone," Professor Kenner has observed, "who in the first decade of this century absorbed and retransmitted the discoveries of Stendhal and Flaubert on an English wavelength."[2] "It was Ford who was able to disengage technique from intuition sufficiently to make useful statements about narrative procedures."[3] Ford's bringing together the French nineteenth-century tradition of fiction with the twentieth-century English novel was part of his effort to remove English intellectual life from its insularity and bring it into what he considered to be the mainstream of European culture.

Ford was one of the great editors of the twentieth century and used his influence as an editor and a literary personality to create a climate that made some of the best writing of the century possible. He founded and edited two literary magazines, the *English Review* in London, from December 1908 to December 1909, and the *transatlantic review* in Paris, from January to December 1924—both as short-lived as they were brilliant. He may not have known what he should have known about the finances of running a magazine, but he had the knack for spotting good writing in a pile of manuscripts from unknown writers. He discovered

D. H. Lawrence, accepting his story "The Odour of Chrysanthemums" after reading no further than the opening paragraph.

The *English Review* has been called "the best literary journal issued in England in this century";[4] it had the best writing of the time—contributions by Thomas Hardy, Henry James, Tolstoy, Conrad, Yeats, H. G. Wells, Pound, Wyndham Lewis, and W. H. Hudson.

In the pages of the *transatlantic review*, Ford published Gertrude Stein, James Joyce, E. E. Cummings, Pound, Conrad, William Carlos Williams, Paul Valéry, John Dos Passos, and Ernest Hemingway, whom Ford made his associate editor before Hemingway had published any of his novels. It was in the *transatlantic review* that Fitzgerald, living in Paris, read Hemingway for the first time.

Ford "passionately wanted great books to be written,"[5] and with little wish for discipleship, he discovered, helped, boosted, and found publishers for "les jeunes"—the young and unknown writers in whom he saw promise—in London in the years before World War I, in Paris in the 1920s, and in New York City in the 1920s and 1930s. Among the American writers he befriended and encouraged were Allen Tate, Caroline Gordon, Katherine Anne Porter, Eudora Welty, William Carlos Williams, and Robert Lowell.

Ford was a real man of letters—"the last great European man of letters," he was called. To the Republic of Letters, as he spoke of it, he contributed children's stories, poetry, history, biography, memoirs, criticism (of society, of literature, and of art), and even propaganda for the Allies in World War I. And he wrote some of the best novels ever written.

Few serious writers, as he himself noted ruefully, have written so many words. "I am, thank you," Ford wrote in a letter in 1910, "well, prosperous and occupied."

With my right hand I am writing a history of cholera in Ireland; with my left an historical novel dealing with the divorce of Anne Boleyn, using it as a peg on which to hang many disquisitions on Divorce in general. My feet are dealing with the treadles of a type-writing machine that pours out the history of literature in England during the last two years, whilst my eyes are engaged in perusing the materials for my gigantic life of Sejanus.

Although he would complain—and Conrad shared with him the complaint as well as the authorship of three books—that writing was *"un métier de chien"* (a dog's occupation) , Ford described himself repeatedly as "a man mad about writing." "Largeness is," as Robert Lowell has put it, "the key word,"[6] and it refers to both Ford's output and his imagination.

Ford never knew how many books he had written; he never counted them or kept copies. When he was asked to explain or discuss them, he often could not, or would not. In a letter in 1933 he wrote:

I am sorry I cannot say more about my books. I hope you will take it that it is because I am like Marcus Aurelius' really virtuous man who, when he had put forth his good works, thought no more of them than does the vine when its grapes are gathered.

In all his critical writing he left us with relatively few direct clues to his novels. But in the immense context his oeuvre provided, there are sudden shafts of light that help the reader with the problems and ambiguities of any single work. In the case of *The Good Soldier*, for example, much of the published criticism suffers from the critics' failure to have read Ford's earlier novels and essays and to pick up the sense of Ford's intentions working themselves out in those books. And in any number of unexpected places—like

the following passage from his little book on Rossetti
—we are given glimpses into the whole direction of
Ford's work, of the whole course of his development
as a novelist:

A great master's art is the art of a man who knows, who has
found out for himself—after pains more or less acute, after
many wasted essays more or less definite in aim, after many
failures felt and learned from—how to produce consum-
mately the impression that he aims at. Rossetti never mas-
tered his instrument.

Or consider Ford's remarks, in his book on Hans
Holbein, of the value of the deliberately simplified
background, remarks which prefigure his use of the
same pictorial principle in *The Good Soldier* and
tell us so much about his particular aesthetic sensibility:

There is here no background, no detailed accessory to worry
the beholder's eye. The figures in the picture exist just as at
first sight a great human individuality exists.

Or take this passage from an unlikely source—his
anti-German *When Blood Is Their Argument*, written
during World War I for the British Ministry of Information—in which he tells us how his imagination
worked. He had read Petronius's *Satyricon*

not so much for its own or any classical sake, as in the
attempt to identify myself with the medieval point of view,
or the renaissance point of view, of things in general. I was
trying, that is to say, to consider how the world [of the sixteenth century] would appear to Katherine Howard.

Katherine was the heroine of Ford's historical
trilogy *The Fifth Queen*, and behind Ford's conception of her lay his effort to consider how the world
could appear to a beautiful and reflective young
woman, very much on her own in the court of Henry
VIII and obliged to make her own analogies in order

to understand it. What interested Ford in respect to
the *Satyricon* was the kind of analogy with her own
world that would have forced itself upon Katherine
in her reading of the grotesqueries of a first-century
Roman banquet. Ford's historical and psychological
imagination required him to read with and through
the eyes of his characters: how we read a book is tan-
tamount to how we read the world.

Ford had great admiration for a little-known
French novelist, René Béhaine, who he sometimes
claimed was the greatest living novelist. It was a case
of elective affinities: Béhaine "also has been writing
one masterpiece for upwards of twenty years and, . . .
heaven help us, is quite as unpopular as . . . I." Béhaine's series of novels (which started about the same
time as Ford's) belonged to an overarching conception, and he subsumed them all under the title *L'his-
toire d'une société*. As a novelist, he clearly belonged
to the category Proust spoke of in connection with
Hardy and Dostoievsky, prolific writers whose di-
versity of books is only apparent: all their books are
in reality one gigantic book. A recent critic of Proust
has commented interestingly on this idea.

Even in a novel by Hardy or Dostoievsky the complications
of the plot are only incidental, only a strategy, so to speak,
whereby the unique world of these writers can take on form
and permanence. That is why we can say that all novelists,
even the most prolific, have really only written one book,
which in the case of Dostoievsky should be called *Crime and
Punishment*, in the case of Flaubert, *L'Education Senti-
mentale*.[7]

Pound would ask Ford from time to time if he was
ever getting his *real* book finished, and as late as 1927,
Ford still wanted to write "one good book."
    Instead of laboring for years over a single book,
bringing it to perfection as Flaubert, for example, did,

Ford on the whole (though there is evidence of a good deal of rewriting) "corrected" through a new version, a new novel. "Great writers," he once remarked, "or strong personalities, when they have passed their impressionable years, are no longer subject to influences. They develop along lines of their own geniuses." Ford was such a writer, though he would have hedged about calling himself great. The point I wish to make is that he worked and reworked the basic material of his imagination—images, characters, situations—and that each reworking was only an approximation of the ideal novel that eluded him.

He often applied the image of cat's cradle, the string game, to his method of construction: ". . . to get any pattern at all out of these confusions," he explained in *Provence*, one of his last books, "it is necessary to go through them several times from different angles." Roughly speaking, he used this method in all his books—those he frankly called fiction and those he called memoirs, biography, sociological impressions, etc. The idea of reworking the same material from different angles lent itself to his special genius for the psychological novel, and in some way, he conceived every book he wrote as a psychological novel. Curiously, the image of cat's cradle seems appropriate for the whole of his output as well as the individual books.

As early as his first fairy tale, Ford used cat's cradle as a metaphor for reading. The princess in *The Feather* (1892) "tried playing cat's cradle by herself; but that was not a very great success, because there was no one to take it up." As the princess realizes, she is playing a game that needs two players; the pattern depends on two pairs of hands. The reader of Ford's books has his part to play, or the whole fabric, carefully built up, loses its coherence and comes undone. The game, which Ford intended the reader to play with seriousness and pleasure, referred to more than technique. It had to do with the purpose of art as Ford understood it.

For the province of literature is to educate, so that the reader may be stirred to the perception of analogies or to the discovery of the sources of pleasure within himself. It is for that you go to the Arts, and for no other purpose.[8]

2

~~~~~~~~~~~~~~~~~~~~~~~~~~~~~~~~~~~

His Life

Ford was born in 1873, to a family distinguished for its part in the artistic and musical life of England. His grandfather was the painter Ford Madox Brown. His uncles by marriage* were the editor and writer William Michael Rossetti and the poet and painter Dante Gabriel Rossetti. The poet Christina Rossetti, their sister, preferring accuracy, called Ford "my dear young connection" rather than nephew; and Ford's sense of connection, never very simple and on the whole rather uneasy, with the Rossetti family, was to become a significant fact in the shaping of his attitude toward art and toward himself.

Ford's father, Ernest Hueffer, was a musicologist, the leading music critic for *The Times* of London, and the earliest champion of Wagner's music in England. The households in which Ford grew up—both his father's and, after his death, the grandfather's—provided an atmosphere in which it was assumed that a life spent in the service of art was not only the best of all possible lives but the only possible life. There were almost too many examples of such a life before Ford:

---

* Ford's mother, Catherine Madox Brown, was Ford Madox Brown's daughter by a second marriage. Her half-sister Lucy, the child of Brown's first wife, married William Michael Rossetti, brother of Dante Gabriel and Christina.

the eminent Victorians whom he saw at first hand as
visitors and acquaintances of the family; Dante Gabriel and Christina Rossetti, opposing types as personalities and artists; and the grandfather whom Ford
loved and admired. Ford had, therefore, a very strong
dose of nineteenth-century high-mindedness—and
rather mixed feelings about his own part in such a
world.

His earliest memories, as he tells us in his autobiographical books, were of sinfulness and clumsiness.[1]
His father had called him "the patient but extremely
stupid donkey," and his younger brother, Oliver,
seemed quicker and more successful, leaving Ford
with the mental set of the younger brother—overshadowed and second-best. "From my earliest days I
was taught . . . to regard him as the sparkling jewel
of the family, while I was its ugly duckling."

Throughout his life Ford spoke of himself as an
animal, mostly of the large and unwieldy kind—ele-
phant, behemoth, buffalo—and as a child he was
"timid" and "incapable of assertion." His Rossetti
cousins were "horrible monsters of precocity." Stimu-
lated by the "educational fury" of their mother, Ford's
Aunt Lucy, who believed that "work, work, work, was
the object of life," the children published an anarchist
newspaper in their basement. "I had four cousins
who, though they were young, were social reformers,"
Ford's sister Juliet wrote later.[2] They also produced
plays in which Ford took part, feeling very foolish
("Speak up, Fordie!") ; the cousins seemed generally
to set a standard he felt he could not hope to meet.

With adults he felt even more ill at ease: adults
were the mysterious "they," powers that represented
restraints of all sorts:

For you ought to consider that upon the one hand as a
child I was very severely disciplined, and, when I was not

being severely disciplined, I moved among somewhat distinguished people who all appeared to me to be morally and
physically twenty-five feet high.

These distinguished people were the great Victorian and Pre-Raphaelite writers and artists who fre-
quented his grandfather's house and to whom he was,
as a very small child, presented. They were "nearly as
often in the house itself, as are in England such ordinary household things as Black's mustard, Dash's
Worcestershire sauce. . . ." But Ford never got used
to the distinguished persons.

. . . There were in those days a number of those terrible
and forbidding things—the Victorian great figures. To me
life was simply not worth living because of the existence
of Carlyle, of Mr. Ruskin, of Mr. Holman Hunt, of Mr.
Browning, or of the gentleman who built the Crystal Palace.
These people were perpetually held up to me as standing
upon unattainable heights, and at the same time I was perpetually being told that if I could not attain these heights
I might just as well not cumber the earth. What then was
left for me? Nothing. Simply nothing.

How small they made him feel, how stupid, how
threatened and oppressed by their immense presences and booming voices and impossibly high ideals
(Ruskin's "power and eloquence as a speaker were
Homeric") ; all of these sensations felt by the child
should have produced a lifelong discomfort with the
great Victorians, and they did. Yet Ford always had
an intense sense of belonging to the nineteenth century. A good deal of his later critical animus against
the Victorian novel may have derived from these early
feelings; but in spite of them he was indebted to and
fascinated by the Victorians. Not only did they give
him what he so needed—something to rebel against
(as he could not rebel against his parents or his grandfather who seemed so "advanced") , but Victorian

thought and art provided ideas and attitudes, innovations and patterns, with which his own work was
continuous: he felt rooted in the nineteenth century.

Ford was twenty-seven when the new century
began; his life span encompassed the literary generations from John Ruskin's to Robert Lowell's. Ford
belonged to a generation of writers—Proust, Gide,
Mann, Yeats, Joyce—that sounded the modern note
in literature most authoritatively; all of them had a
special awareness of time that derived from living in
two centuries, and their work is very much a record
of the relationship between those two centuries. Henry
Adams's complaint—"It was a mistake to have been
born in the nineteenth century when the whole of
your life was to be passed in the twentieth"—helps us
to understand the sense of homelessness such writers
felt. The experience of time and the process of change
came to be one of the great permanent subjects of
the new literature Ford helped to create.

His father, born Franz Karl Christoph Johann
Hüffer, left his prosperous family of printers and
publishers in Germany to settle in London. There,
Dr. Francis Hueffer, as he was called (he had a German doctorate and had studied with Schopenhauer),
started the *New Quarterly Review* to promote Schopenhauer in England; as Ford observed pointedly
after his own experience as an editor, the review
caused his father "to lose a great deal of money and
to make cordial enemies among the poets and literary men to whom he gave friendly lifts." Francis
Hueffer married Catherine Madox Brown, the
younger daughter of Ford Madox Brown. As a wed-
ding present the Carlyles gave the young couple a
writing desk; not long afterward, Dante Gabriel Rossetti wrote a limerick about Francis Hueffer which
Ford quoted in *Ancient Lights*.

There was a young German called Huffer,
A hypochondriacal buffer;
    To shout Schopenhauer
    From the top of a tower
Was the highest enjoyment of Huffer.

He had other enjoyments as well. Among the visitors to his house was Franz Liszt: Ford remembered shaking hands "with a clergyman called Franz Liszt." And so respected was Dr. Hueffer as a critic of music that Queen Victoria once sent him a note from her box at Covent Garden, asking for his opinion of the strange opera then being performed. She was hearing Wagner for the first time.

The limerick leaves no doubt about the pronunciation of Hueffer; the hypochondria may have had a basis in physical fact. In January 1889, when Ford was sixteen, his father died of a heart attack. He left behind very little money, three children, and an injunction that his son never heeded: "Fordie, whatever you do, never write a book." Hueffer himself had written a great deal: an important book on Wagner, numerous translations and articles, three librettos for operas that were set to music and produced. He had edited the Wagner-Liszt correspondence (which is once again in print) and an extensive series of volumes called *The Great Musicians*. But his most important work was *The Troubadours, a History of Provençal Life and Literature in the Middle Ages*, according to Ford "the first continuous and at all adequate account in the English language" of that subject.

Francis Hueffer's study of the troubadours awakened and sustained the interest of several decades of readers, laying the groundwork for many of the translations and studies that followed, Pound's included. Ford's pride in *The Troubadours* is clear: "He was . . . in his day the greatest authority upon the trou-

badours and the Romance Languages." Of all the
attitudes Dr. Hueffer imparted to his son, perhaps
his love for Provence and its poetry, an art of great
formal elaborateness, was the most significant. Hueffer had defined the troubadour as

a representative of art, or if the reader prefers it, artificiality, in its strictest and most highly developed sense. The
metres invented and used with consummate skill by the
poets of medieval Provence remain a marvel of symmetry
and technical perfection in the history of literature, unequalled by the poets of other nations. . . .[3]

The father's statement was to define what the
son would try to achieve in the novel. Ford's real,
and perhaps his only ambition (by his own account
he was not an ambitious man), was to write the kind
of novel a troubadour poet might have written, in
which the pleasure to be derived from the writing lay
in the most refined perception of the uses of pattern.

To the end of their lives, both Ford and his sister Juliet thought of themselves not as the children of
their parents but as primarily the grandchildren of
Ford Madox Brown, the painter. It was, as we say now,
the extended rather than the nuclear family that left
its imprint on their imagination. For one thing,
Madox Brown invited his daughter and her children
to come and live with him after Francis Hueffer's
death, and the two households merged very happily.
Madox Brown, according to Juliet in her delightful
book *Chapters from Childhood*, was "one of the kindest, gentlest, handsomest old gentlemen that ever
lived";[4] Ford described him as looking like the King
of Hearts in a pack of cards, "with his square white
beard and his long white hair cut square." He was
"extravagantly indulgent" with his grandchildren and
adored by them. Ford was very young when he came

to appreciate how remarkable his grandfather was: he was as dedicated to his art and to the life that art enforces—work, stubbornness, idealism—as it was possible to be. In short, Madox Brown was a believer in what used to be spoken of as the priestly calling of art. Observant as he was, Ford could find no inconsistencies in this respect, no hypocrisies or meannesses. He would look in vain "for a more chivalrous, benevolent, and Christian man in all the world." And as an old man, in the midst of writing his misunderstood last novels, Ford wrote in *Provence* about his grandfather: "He must have been seventy—and still experimenting as all artists must do to the end of their days if they do not wish to die from the root upwards."

On his side, the grandfather had had great hopes for his remarkably gifted son, Oliver Madox Brown (after whom Ford's brother was named), who died mysteriously at eighteen, when Ford was a baby. The loss had a good deal to do with the old man's expectations of his grandchildren. "My grandfather had to have geniuses for his grandchildren," and Ford felt himself to have been "trained for genius," with his grandfather pushing the influential Edward Garnett into arrangements for the publication of Ford's first book, *The Brown Owl*, a fairy tale he had written at eighteen to amuse Juliet. To ensure its success, the grandfather illustrated it with two of his drawings; later, Ford was to say that *The Brown Owl* had sold better than anything else he ever published.

From Ford's point of view, Madox Brown was his real father—a more perfect, more permanent, less rigid and much older father than his own—and one who regarded Ford not as a patient and exceedingly stupid donkey, but as a genius. The grandfather provided perhaps the one element in his life to which he did not respond ambiguously. Madox Brown is the

undisputed hero of Ford's autobiographical writings.
(Ford himself is at best the disputable hero.) The
sense of identification Ford felt with him was almost
complete: the old man with his Inverness around his
shoulders, the young man dressing like his grandfather, being very old and wise, taking his younger
sister to visit the Russian anarchist Prince Kropotkin,
who was living in London. Juliet remembered Ford as

a fair, clever young man, rather scornful, with smooth pink
cheeks and a medium-sized hooked nose like my grandfather's, a high, intellectual forehead, and quiet, absent-
looking blue eyes that seemed as if they were always pon-
dering over something. I was nervous with him, because he
was very critical and thought that nearly every one was stupid and not worth disagreeing with. But he was very kind
and liked to take me out to tea. He wore a black coat with
a cape over the shoulders, and when we took hands and
walked along it floated out a little way behind.[5]

Ford, who enjoyed "analyzing" his heredity, liked to
think he had inherited even his grandfather's faults:
"Nothing can prevent my mixing up names. I suppose
I inherit the characteristic from my grandfather who
had it to a dangerous degree."

At twenty-three, after Madox Brown's death, Ford
was asked to write the book that his grandfather de-
served—*Ford Madox Brown, A Record of His Life
and Work*. Perhaps for the first time, Ford had deliberately to offset his strong feelings of identification
and write "in as critical and unimpassioned a manner as I could command." It was a discipline that
taught him a great deal about keeping the proper
distance from his subject.

Ford's final assessment of his grandfather was
uncannily prophetic: did Ford "inherit" the pattern
of his grandfather's life?

During a long life he received little honour, and few honours, and was in some ways a singularly unlucky man. But he managed to work on, to do good work, and, as he quaintly phrased it, 'to go to bed with both ears on.'

Moreover, he remained to the end of his life young in mind, and, that being so, perhaps the gods loved him after all.

He did catch from his grandfather his flair for telling stories—the picturesque inaccuracies, with their rewarding kernel of truth, the theme inside the variations. Juliet reported:

My grandfather told stories so well that some people said he did it better than anybody else in London, and you never got tired of them because they were a little different each time.[6]

There were always listeners: Madox Brown's house was "a meeting-place for almost all the intellectual unconventional of that time," and Ford remained convinced all of his life of the value of a community of artists. The brotherhood of poets and painters that called itself the Pre-Raphaelites formed such a union, and it was for this reason Ford admired them, rather than for their poetry and painting: "perhaps in their lives they were greater than in their works." Much of his own energy went into the effort to form a community of writers: behind his celebrated hospitality (he was "as hospitable as Zeus")[7] and the literary magazines (he paid for them out of his own pocket) was the model of his grandfather.

In his early novel *Seraphina*, which became the basis for Ford's and Conrad's *Romance*, Ford makes the young hero an earl's grandson. If Ford felt himself to be something of an aristocrat—as he did—it was at least partly on his grandfather's account. Madox Brown's nobility was a matter of character, not title. An egalitarian aristocrat, he had, as Ford

alienating readers. Ford's judgments were highly personal, often overstated, and deliberately outrageous, but behind them was an unwillingness to corroborate an aesthetic that had already had its day. How he read other writers and how he theorized about his own writing all had to do with his forward-looking momentum: the writer must represent and interpret his own age and look toward the future.

Ford spoke of himself as "not being to the English manner born," a position that gave him a congenital right to be an outsider and observer of English life. If he presented himself as a bona fide English gentleman, as he is reported to have done, he was probably trying out how it felt to be one, and if he suggested that he had been to Winchester or Eton, it was because he took "with extraordinary seriousness" the spirit of the great English public schools: they were, he wrote in *When Blood Is Their Argument*, "in many ways the finest product of a civilization," with their "traditions of responsibilities, duties, privileges, and no rights."

Ford did not go to Winchester or Eton; he went to Praetoria House in the south of England, a coeducational and rather experimental school run by Dr. and Mrs. Praetorius, German friends of his grandfather and former students of Froebel, the German educational philosopher who founded the kindergarten system. Ford also attended University College School in London. Both before and after his father's death, he made frequent trips to the Continent, staying once in Provence with his father's friend, the poet Frédéric Mistral, and later with various members of the Hueffer family, attending lectures on agriculture at the Sorbonne and studying history at the University of Bonn. The fact that he had two other cultures—French and German—with which to identify himself (though of the two, he felt far more strongly drawn to the French), accentuated his feelings about being only partly an Englishman.

There were other difficulties as well, and deciding on a profession was one. His comment that the Pre-Raphaelites were perhaps greater in their lives than in their works reveals how much the question of a profession represented a fundamental choice for him; it was not a matter of hitting upon one field rather than another or of finally acceding to his grandfather's expectations, but of deciding on which was to be more important—his life or his work. Later, in *No Enemy*, he was to write: "The real lives of men are enshrined in their products." That he felt himself by nature to be "a man usually of action" made the decision to be a writer all the more complicated. (His enlistment in the army during World War I when he was over forty, searing as the experience was, in some basic way seemed finally to satisfy that part of him.)

He had been trained in music, having studied composition and violin, but he seemed to know his own capacities and the requirements of musical life well enough to put aside the idea of being a profes-sional musician. He did have an ear; it was a remark-able ear for all kinds of speech, which he could tran-scribe delightfully, getting down its rhythms and its notes, as if he were writing music. But he also thought of going to sea, of being a good sailor, like his great-grandfather, Ford Brown, who had been a naval offi-cer in the Napoleonic wars. Ford had immense respect for the traditions of the sea, which, he felt, enjoined a purity compared to which "the virtues of the sol-dier . . . are crimes." To do a shipshape job of any-thing, he said repeatedly, was the highest good.

No wonder he and Conrad took to one another when they met.

My affection for Conrad was so great and remains so un-
changed that I have never been able really to believe in his
death, and at this moment it is as if he was sitting behind
me waiting to read what I have tapped out. You see, we
did live together, day in day out, for many years—ten, I
daresay and even towards the end he could not really get
on without me any more than I could or can get ob [sic]
without him. . . .[8]

From 1898, when Ford was twenty-five and Conrad was forty, the two men began a collaboration that
carried them "officially" through ten years and three
novels—*The Inheritors* (1901), *Romance* (1904),
and *The Nature of a Crime* (published in 1909 in
the *English Review*, in 1924 in the *transatlantic review*, and as a book in 1924). During the period of
their collaboration, each man continued to write his
own books as well. Long afterward, and in another
context altogether, Ford quoted the German writer
Novalis: "It is certain that my conviction gains im-
mensely as soon as another soul can be found to share
it."[9] Conrad was that other soul, and the two men
offered one another the sense of community they
strongly missed in English literary life: an experience
of shared passion and shared assumptions about art,
particularly the art of the novel as it had been prac-
ticed by Flaubert and Maupassant and Turgenev.
"We agreed that the novel is absolutely the only ve-
hicle for the thought of our day. With the novel you
can do anything." They conversed in French, set
themselves fictional exercises, and recited long passages from Flaubert and Maupassant, as other men
might recite poetry. Conrad "used to say that he had
made the decision to write in English in Rouen har-
bour, opposite the hotel in which Emma Bovary had
been accustomed to meet Rodolphe." The French
novel—and English prose—became their "religion."

What the two writers learned from the French

novelists and from one another is more important
than either the sum of the three novels they wrote
together or the question of who wrote which part of
what book. A reasonable assessment puts it that their
collaboration was "extensive in . . . *The Inheritors*
. . . or *Romance* . . . , less extensive but present to
some degree in works which we think of as more properly Conrad's such as *Lord Jim* (1900), *Typhoon*
(1902), *Nostromo* (1904), and the short stories 'Falk'
or 'Amy Foster.' "[10]

Conrad had come to Ford on the advice of
friends: he needed help in writing for an English
audience.

My intimate, automatic, less expressed thoughts are in Po-
lish; when I express myself with care I do it in French.
When I write I think in French and then translate the
words of my thoughts into English.*

Ford's analysis, in *Joseph Conrad: A Personal Remembrance* (1924), of Conrad's difficulties with English
may or may not have been correct, but his impression of the immense difficulties Conrad felt as a writer
in English *was* correct. Conrad felt himself to be
floundering and blocked, in real doubt about himself as a writer in English, writing so slowly and
with such "torture" that he needed help, both lexical
and psychological. Ford gave him the help he needed.
He loosened up Conrad's bookish English, acted for
him as "a sort of thesaurus—a handy dictionary of

---

* Compare Ford's account of his own relation to language in his preface to *When Blood Is Their Argument*:
". . . Whenever I have thought with great care of a prose
paragraph, I have framed it in my mind in French, or more
rarely in Latin, and have then translated into English;
whereas when it was a matter of such attempts at verse as
I have made, my thinking has been done exclusively in col-
loquial English."

synonyms," directed him "towards an easy use of
the vernacular," the really living language that had
eluded Conrad (that "more fluid language in which
words assimilate themselves to each other with deli-
cacy and tenuity.") More importantly, Ford nursed
him through illnesses real and imagined, cajoled him
into writing, took it all down in shorthand once the
flow started, housed him and his family, lent him
money, took care of his business affairs—tried, in
short, to relieve Conrad's suffering ("Few men can
so much have suffered") as far as he could and make
it possible for him to write.

On his side, Ford got from Conrad what he most
needed. As H. G. Wells pointed out, Ford had been
"a little undecided between music, poetry, criticism,
The Novel, Thoreau-istic horticulture and the simple
appreciation of life.[11] Conrad helped him to focus his
energies and define his calling and was probably the
most important influence on his work until *The Good
Soldier*. "But for him," Ford wrote in a letter in
1920, "I should have been a continuation of Dante
Gabriel Rossetti."

As novelists they complemented one another.

The differences in our temperaments were sufficiently well
marked. Conrad was brave: he was for inclusion and hang
the consequences. The writer [Ford], more circumspect, was
for ever on the watch to suppress the melodramatic incident
and the sounding phrase.

Conrad's instincts were more "architectonic" than
Ford's; he knew better how to build a story up, had
those "special muscles" for timing and control, could
make of each sentence "a mosaic of little crepitations
of surprise," with every paragraph containing its little
jolt. Conrad could paint with broader strokes than
Ford, and the strong painterly quality of his imagination strengthened the visual element in Ford's work.

Ford tended to be more analytic in narration, and under Conrad's influence he did not become less so; he became more graphic as well. Conrad made him "see things freshly," and together they shared "constatations of some exactness" long after their collaboration ended. In his letters from the front (1916), Ford sent him notes on sounds: the quality of sounds in different kinds of terrain—woody country, marshland, clay land—in different kinds of weather. It was the kind of thing they both cared about enormously.

In all their "10,000 conversations" during their years together, there were, Ford reported, only two matters for quarreling: the taste of saffron and whether one sheep is distinguishable from another. For almost a decade, they worked "with absolute oneness of purpose and with absolute absence of rivalry" (Ford's statement) —except, perhaps, in their competitiveness over which of them suffered more from illness and nerves. But Mrs. Conrad deeply resented her husband's total absorption in what seemed to be an intimacy that excluded her.* The difficulties that inhered in the relationship all around were for Ford just the "rubs of the game," and there was no question for him about the value of playing it. Professor Hynes has pointed out that Conrad "worked his young partner cruelly hard . . . and on occasion ridiculed him behind his back; in later years he referred to Ford in the most denigrating terms."[12] Yet Ford's view of the relationship seemed quite free of pettiness or resentment; only

---

* Nor was she really comfortable with Ford's wife, Elsie, who was clearly better educated than she (and published in 1903 a translation of Maupassant's stories with a preface by Ford). Jessie nevertheless took the occasion of Ford's later estrangement from Elsie and his affair with Violet Hunt to voice loud disapproval of his morals, a position in which Conrad concurred.

the note of pain is there and the great admiration for "miraculous gifts."

"I must in the old days have accompanied his mind through at least a million written words and as many more that never got onto paper." Conversely, "during all those years, the writer [Ford] wrote every word that he wrote, with the idea of reading aloud to Conrad." Their relationship was "curiously impersonal"—two English gentlemen, the one "bobbing stiffly to the other, like mandarins," Conrad's "Oriental" elaborateness and courtesy transposed into the English manner.

But Ford saw himself and Conrad in another way, too, and that is perhaps the most interesting part of the story. Conrad may have been an English gentleman, but he was also a Pole, and as Ford's logic went, therefore an Elizabethan. "Conrad is Renaissance, because Poland is a sixteenth century nation—and we want all the Renaissance stuff we can get in these islands." What Ford prized in Conrad was his "passion" and "chivalry" and "fidelity." In short, Ford was willing to be his squire, to do Conrad's "literary dustings and sweepings," to be his "lifelong habit." Their relationship became one of the central facts of Ford's consciousness as a novelist, and at the end of the book on Conrad, he wrote: "moi-même sûrement son Sancho" ("and I surely his Sancho"). It followed that Conrad was therefore Don Quixote—"le dernier Don Quixote de la Manza du mot juste en Angleterre" ("the last Don Quixote of the *mot juste* in England"). All of these perceptions about himself and Conrad went into the making of *The Good Soldier*, with its primary relationship—between the narrator John Dowell and the protagonist Edward Ashburnham—absorbing the Don Quixote-Sancho Panza theme.

How much more complicated the whole matter

seems when we remember how fascinated Ford was
with Conrad's capacity for writing two opposite kinds
of fiction—novels like *The Secret Agent,* set in London, and novels like *Nostromo,* set in exotic places. It
was a polarity in Conrad's nature that paralleled
Ford's own. And it was inevitable that their starting
point as collaborators should have been entitled *Romance,* as if they needed to define their use of the
term at the very outset and signal their agreement in
capital letters.

Ford wrote his book on Conrad during the two
months that followed Conrad's death in 1924. It was,
as Ford said

a projection of Joseph Conrad as, little by little, he revealed
himself to a human being during many years of close intimacy. It is so that, by degrees, Lord Jim appeared to
Marlow, or that every human soul by degrees appears to
every other human soul.

The most fitting way Ford could honor Conrad was
to turn a biographical essay into a novel.

A good deal of Ford's material as a novelist presented itself to him ominously and with unsettling
velocity in the years before World War I, when everything in his personal world seemed to fall apart as
Europe headed for war. For complex financial and
literary-political reasons, Ford lost the editorship of
the *English Review.* And there was a scandal of immense proportions over his attempted divorce from
Elsie Martindale, whom he had married when he was
twenty-one and she was seventeen, and with whom he
had two daughters. His liaison with Violet Hunt, a
well-known literary personality (D. H. Lawrence
"rather" liked her—"she's such a real assassin": "the
hooks are through his [Ford's] gills") [13] compounded

both the legal difficulties and the publicity that the
trial was given. For a man who instinctively hated
scenes and shrank from them in private life, the episode was deeply humiliating and left him with a feeling of "contamination" and a nervous dread of seeing
his name in the newspapers. Friends of long standing,
among them Conrad and Henry James, showed their
disapproval by falling away. (His relationship with
James had never been comfortable: Ford felt that
James never had him correctly in focus, and the person James put into Merton Densher in *The Wings of
the Dove* was never the person Ford perceived himself
to be—nor was he simply *"le jeune homme modeste,"*
as James used to call him.)

Both the magazine and the attempted divorce,
which his wife never did grant, exhausted him finan-
cially. In the bankruptcy that followed—and in the
separation from his two small daughters, to whom he
was greatly attached—he experienced a sense of almost total loss. How to objectify so much pain and
self-pity and self-justification, how to produce order
out of such disarray occupied him in what must have
been a feverish process. He wrote sixteen books between 1910 and 1915, through them all moving away,
in as many directions as possible, from the personal
trauma and toward the absolute control of *The Good
Soldier*, where the pressure of two orders of events,
personal and public, is transmitted on every page,
and the tension between them perfectly sustained.

In 1915, Ford enlisted in the British Army, "too
old for that job." That no one wrote to him when he
was at the front was his most recurrent complaint in
his letters: it was like being a ghost. He lived through
the war, the "nerve-tangle of war," including the
Battle of the Somme, and came out of it with the sense
of having died. His "once prodigious" memory was

lost after he had been gassed. Once he had been able, he reported, to sit down and not translate but write out in French all of *The Good Soldier* from memory. Now he was "deliriously" unable to remember names.

Professor Kenner's statement—"Civilization is memory, and after 1918 effective memory was almost lost"[14]—suggests why so much twentieth-century fiction is concerned with memory, the very technique of the novel becoming an instrument for recovering the past. Again the world debacle paralleled Ford's own; and again the books he wrote, most notably *No Enemy*, *The Marsden Case*, and *Parade's End*, drew their strength from that unhappy connection. World War I was another of the great facts of Ford's consciousness. *The Good Soldier*, dealing by implication with the outset of the war, and *Parade's End*, treating the years before, during, and after the war, are conceived as patterns of memory, both voluntary and involuntary.

"That vast amnesia,"[15] Professor Kenner's phrase for World War I, left Ford with the impression that his life had been broken in half: he would have to will the second half into existence. He returned to "a strange London" in early 1919, to find that as a writer he had been "completely forgotten." "Naked came I from my mother's womb," he later quoted when he described his feelings at that time. The change of name to the odd and circular Ford Madox Ford was an effort to reconstruct himself, make new beginnings, perhaps make ends and beginnings one and the same. The sense of displacement he had suffered—after the suffering of the war—was on the whole confirmed until he decided to leave England permanently in 1922.

About nine months before the Armistice, Ford met and fell in love with the young Australian painter

Stella Bowen.* Together they tried, gallantly, to live
in a succession of leaky-roofed cottages in Sussex, Ford
farming and suffering from ill health, and under
Stella's encouragement, beginning again to write.

Their move, with their daughter Julie, to the south
of France and then Paris, opened a new phase in
Ford's life. In Paris he greatly enjoyed the way of life
that went with the editorship of the *transatlantic review*—the literary activity, the chance to be an "influence," the parties he and Stella gave in their studio,
and the *bal musette*, the little café he rented on Fri-
days to serve as open house. (Hemingway put this
café into *The Sun Also Rises*, along with rather mali-
cious portraits of Ford and Stella as Mr. and Mrs.
Braddocks.†) Ford would dance to the accordion—"a
tall mountain of a man," Stella wrote later in *Drawn
from Life*, "whose dancing was never more than an
amiable shuffle." When the review folded, because
"his whole system rejected any knowledge of money
matters," his anguish, very real, was offset by what was
apparent to both Stella and Ford: that he was embark-
ing on "the best creative work of his life," and that the
new work (the novels making up *Parade's End*) could
absorb his disappointment and sustain him.

---

* Ford's disengagement from Violet Hunt was not easy,
and she proved tenacious. The seeds of discord were clearly
visible in Ford's corrective—and impatient—footnotes to
her hasty, superficial impressions of Germany in their joint
effort *The Desirable Alien*. By 1918, differences in temperament, in age (she was—and looked—much older than he),
in attitude toward the war, were all the more sharply defined by the changes in Ford caused by his experience of the
war.

† "Hemingway, as is well known, virulently hated
everybody who had ever done anything for him in his
youth." This comment by Kenneth Rexroth was made in
his introduction to Ford's *Buckshee*.

In 1924, while Ford was living with Stella Bowen in Paris, he met Jean Rhys. Destitute, friendless, and serious about writing, she showed the manuscript of her first novel to him and Stella. They befriended her, offering her the spare room they had offered to other starving writers; this time, the arrangement became a *ménage à trois*, and the situation found its way into Miss Rhys's novel *Postures* (published in 1928 and called *Quartet* in the American edition of 1929). Both Hugh Heidler in *Postures* and Mr. Mackenzie in the sequel to it, *After Leaving Mr. Mackenzie* (1931), are Miss Rhys's versions of Ford, and neither portrait is very flattering. Ford is presented as selfish, unfeeling, indifferent to the heroine's situation; he wants simply to discharge his debt and disengage himself.

Ford's version of the affair is unknown, but the facts are that he and Stella, far from leaving Miss Rhys destitute, settled on her an allowance that was to continue, as Professor Mizener has determined, long after she left—"at least until the end of 1926."[16] Ford then wrote a twenty-page preface to her collection of stories *The Left Bank* (1927) to help launch her—at a time when he could still draw upon his influence as former editor of the *transatlantic*. Ford also arranged for her to do a translation of Francis Carco's *Perversity* (1928), which he himself had originally undertaken. But Covici, the publisher, conveniently forgetting that Ford had not himself done the translation, attributed it to Ford ("because they thought it would sell better," Ford suspected), and Miss Rhys was not given credit.

Ford's intention—to help her get started on a literary career—and his good faith were clear enough in his preface to her stories. His praise is generous:

Setting aside for a moment the matter of her very remarkable technical gifts, I should like to call attention to her

profound knowledge of the life of the Left Bank—of the
Left Banks of the world.

And his claims for her are somewhat overstated:

What struck me on the technical side . . . was the singular
instinct for form possessed by this young lady, an instinct
for form being possessed by singularly few writers of English
and by almost no English women writers.

Noting her intentional omission of any sort of topography in her stories, Ford commended her for it:
"Her business was with passion, hardship, emotions:
the locality in which these things are endured is im-
material." Yet he devoted most of his preface to his
own impressions of the Latin Quarter, as if to make
up for what she had left out. "But I, knowing for my
sins, the book market, imagined the reader saying:
'Where did all this take place? What sort of places
are these?' So I have butted in."

A contemporary reviewer in the *Times Literary
Supplement* commented engagingly:

In his interesting preface Mr. Ford writes with easy authority about the particular qualities of Parisian Bohemianism,
and his slightly consultatory air, as of a specialist called in
suddenly for an important diagnosis, is distinctly pleasing.
By comparison, Miss Rhys's sketches and short character
studies seem almost tentative.[17]

But there was nothing tentative about the bitterness
behind *Postures*, which had for its epigraph some
lines by R. C. Dunning that began "Beware / Of good
Samaritans. . . ." (Dunning too had been published
by Ford.) In fact, the whole episode abounds in
ironies.

Stella's version of the affair is to be found in her
book *Drawn from Life* (1941), now out of print and
hard to come by. It is important that her side of the
story be known, particularly since she neither attacks
Miss Rhys nor defends herself against the rather dam-

aging portrait of herself as Lois in *Postures*. What she says is worth quoting at length:

. . . Ford had fallen in love with a very pretty and gifted young woman. . . . The girl was a really tragic person. . . . Her gift for prose and her personal attractiveness were not enough to ensure her any reasonable life, for on the other side of the balance were bad health, destitution, shattered nerves, an undesirable husband, lack of nationality, and a complete absence of any desire for independence. . . .

She lived with us for many weeks whilst we tried to set her on her feet. Ford gave her invaluable help with her writing, and I tried to help her with her clothes. I was singularly slow in discovering that she and Ford were in love. . . .

She had a needle-quick intelligence and a good sort of emotional honesty, but she was a doomed soul, violent and demoralised. She had neither the wish nor the capacity to tackle practical difficulties. . . .

She . . . showed us an underworld of darkness and disorder [with] the fugitive the only hero. All the virtues, in her view, were summed up in "being a sport," which meant being willing to take risks and show gallantry and share one's last crust. . . .

. . . Here I was cast for the role of the fortunate wife who held all the cards, and the girl for that of the poor, brave, and desperate beggar, who was doomed to be let down by the bourgeoisie. I learnt what a powerful weapon lies in weakness and pathos and how strong is the position of the person who has nothing to lose, and I simply hated my role! I played it, however, until the girl was restored to health and her job [in the south of France] materialised, since we appeared to represent her last chance of survival. . . .

The eventual waning of Ford's attachment to this girl had its distressing side. A man seldom shows to advantage when trying to get rid of a woman who has become an incubus.

The relationship between Ford and Stella could not remain as it had been: the "fundamental tie" had

been "cut." Ironically, what followed was Stella's recognition that she must have a separate existence from
Ford and a life of her own as a painter: "to realise
that there can be no such thing as 'belonging' to another person (for in the last resort you must be responsible for yourself, just as you must prepare to die
alone), is surely a necessary part of an adult's education!"

Ford was a "great user-up of other people's nervous energy," Stella wrote; with him she was emotion-
ally "on duty twenty-four hours a day," shielding him
from the stresses and business of everyday life so that
he could write. She was ready to build a new life "out
of the ashes of her life with Ford" and develop her
own art. Three years after the Jean Rhys episode they
separated, with Stella in much the same circumstances
the younger woman had been, having to struggle to
make an independent life for herself as a woman and
artist.

Ford's admiration of Jean Rhys's writing had fo-
cused on her "terrific—an almost lurid!—passion for
stating the case of the underdog," as he wrote in his
preface. Ironically, in *Postures*, Mr. Heidler is "top
dog." Miss Rhys's reduction of character and role to
these two categories is interestingly at variance with
the way Stella saw (and she was undeniably influenced by Ford's novelistic habits): "The loftiest wisdom," she wrote, "ought surely to be able to see every
side of everything simultaneously. . . . It belongs to a
state of health and equilibrium. . . . The effective
person says that 'only one thing matters'—but everything matters all the time."

Julia Martin, Miss Rhys's heroine, sees Mr. Mackenzie as "inscrutable" and "invulnerable." Stella
wrote:

Poor Ford! There was something about the sight of his
large patient fingers tapping at the keys, that I always

found infinitely touching. He was a writer—a complete writer—and nothing but a writer. And he never even felt sure of his gift!

He needed more reassurance than anyone I have ever met.

And again Stella on Ford:

The stiff, rather alarming exterior, and the conventional, omniscient manner, concealed a highly complicated emotional machinery. It produced an effect of tragic vulnerability; tragic because the scope of his understanding and the breadth of his imagination had produced a great edifice which was plainly in need of more support than was inherent in the structure itself. A walking temptation to any woman, had I but known it!

The heroine of *Postures* charges Hugh Heidler with despising love. Here is Stella:

I don't think his personal relationships were important at all. They always loomed very large in his own view, but they were not intrinsically important. I don't think it matters much from whom the artist gets his nourishment, or his shelter, so long as he gets it.

In order to keep his machinery running, he requires to exercise his sentimental talents from time to time upon a new object. It keeps him young. It refreshes his ego. It restores his belief in his powers. And who shall say that this type of lubrication is too expensive for so fine a machine?

What strikes the reader is the closeness of Miss Rhys's identification as a novelist with the special consciousness of her heroine (and it is, of course, her special strength as a writer to project it so successfully) , that of a temperament essentially passive, "soft and thin-skinned," clinging, even parasitic—forced to live independently and unable to do it. Locked into categories of dominance and debasement, Miss Rhys sees experience simply and externally, no less so than

her heroines see it, and with no distance from their
bitterness and self-pity. Stella's account is lacking in
either bitterness or self-pity; she seems to have seen
the three sides of the affair from a remarkably large
perspective—more like the wisdom we expect from a
novelist.

After the separation from Stella, Ford made a
succession of trips to the United States, where he was,
according to Stella, "alone and hard-up." He had
never regarded England as his own country, but he
never found a permanent substitute after he left it—
Provence, perhaps, which he loved ideologically and
historically and as an actual place; New York, perhaps, where he became a literary presence in the late
1920s and 1930s; but neither served as a real home,
and he was, as William Carlos Williams described
him in his poem "To Ford Madox Ford in Heaven,"
"homeless here on earth."

He had lived in a great many houses in the course
of his life. In *Return to Yesterday*, he wrote:

I seem to have leased, bought, inhabited, mended, extended,
patched up, cleaned out more houses, households of furniture, carts, harness, waggon-sheds, plots of ground than
there are years to my life or than would have sufficed for
the lifetime of ten other men.

He understood the special character of each house;
in fact, he wrote a long poem called *A House*, which,
as he made a point of mentioning in his *Collected
Poems* (1936), won the prize that *Poetry* magazine
gave "for the best world poem" in 1921. On the whole,
he never stayed very long in any of the houses he
repaired in his improvising way, before he was on
the move again, traveling lightly, with remarkably
little sense of property. (He would rather have *du
goût*, he said: he would rather have taste.) He loved

luxury and despised comfort because, as he wrote in a letter to Julie in 1935, comfort "deadens one's interest in life—and extinguishes self-respect."

As often as he could, he grew his own food, so that he cultivated two gardens; letters and vegetables were his "double occupation." As he explained in *Return to Yesterday*,

The idea of putting tiny dark objects into the ground fascinates me. Over their germination and growth there is something mysterious and exciting. It is the only clean way of attaining the world's desire. You get something for nothing. Yes, it is the only clean way of adding to your store; the only way by which you can eat your bread without taking it out of another's mouth. I used to think that the arts and letters were also not only creative but non-competitive. An author—*auctor*—added to things and took nothing from anyone.

When he visited William Carlos Williams in Rutherford, New Jersey, Ford asked to be taken to see the truck farms. Here is Williams's description:

. . . Ford, who was looking around, questioned the farmer closely about the cultivation of the lettuce, carrots, dandelion, leeks, peppers, tomatoes and radishes which he was raising. It was all part of his understanding of the particular—and of what should properly occupy and compel a man's mind.[18]

Ford could not always stay to harvest the gardens he had dug and hoed and pruned: "The life, then," as he summed it up, "is one of frustrations; if I had not so constantly travelled, I should have reaped better harvests and written more and better books. . . ." But he had also a sense of completion and shape about his life:

In my hot youth—which wasn't really so torrid—I yearned to be—like Horace, Cervantes, Bunyan, and others—both

poet and soldier; having been them, I find myself to have
become pacifist and prosateur.[19]

Toward the end of his life he taught "comparative literature from the beginning of time to the
moment of speaking" at Olivet College in Michigan,
"a refuge for good writers who are down on their end-
bones," as he wrote in a letter. Olivet, in fact, had a
writing program well in advance of its time, but Ford
was sick, and the climate was wrong for him, and the
midwestern landscape did not seem to cheer him up.

He seemed to have a preternaturally vivid spatial
sense that made his relationship to landscape an immediate and profound psychological fact—a matter
which he often explored with great precision and
subtlety. In England he had suffered at times from
agoraphobia, the fear of open space, at other times
from claustrophobia: England's club armchairs "con-
fine your arms, your hips, your very mind." "I shall
suffocate," he wrote in *Provence*, "if I cannot get to a
hard, hot stone, flat on an iron, parched hillside, looking, between olive, almond and mulberry trunks, over
the Mediterranean. . . ."

Williams as a doctor saw how ill and overworked
Ford was by 1938, how close to death he was when he
set out for Provence from New York in May 1939.
"Only France matters among the nations," he had
written in *No Enemy*. "I will resay it as my eyes close
in death." He was too ill to get further than Deauville, where he died "in want," as Robert Lowell wrote
in his poem on Ford. Only Janice Biala, the painter
with whom Ford had lived very happily since 1930,
and two friends were there to bury him, appropriately,
on a hillside overlooking the sea.

He was spared at least the experience of World
War II that was to break out within a few months.
His death coincided with what seemed to those who
remembered the first war as merely the end of a

long armistice. "Pacifist and prosateur," as he had described himself, he had in his way belonged to his century, and to the one before it, and he bore witness to them.

"The death of Ford Madox Ford," Graham Greene wrote, "was like the obscure death of a veteran—an impossibly Napoleonic veteran, say, whose immense memory spanned the period from Jena to Sedan: he belonged to the heroic age of English fiction and outlived it—yet he was only sixty-six."[20]

3

Some Aspects of the *Oeuvre*

The Historical Novels

"We live in our day, we live in our time," Ford wrote in an essay on modern poetry in 1909, "and he is not a proper man who will not look in the face his day and time." When he wrote his historical novels, no matter in what period he set back the action or how much attention he paid to setting and costume and archaic language, Ford's psychological interest in his characters made them contemporary with his own time: their personalities belonged to the twentieth century. In both his historical novels and his novels of contemporary life, Ford "established a theater," to use Hawthorne's phrase, "for the creatures of his imagination," and the distinction between the two genres was more superficial than actual. Ford himself could never quite get over the feeling he expressed in his book on Conrad that "a historical novel even at best is nothing more than a *tour de force*, a fake more or less genuine in inspiration and workmanship, but none the less a fake." What Ford meant was that historical fiction, in using a ready-made set of conventions, developed and exhausted by the writers of an earlier time, was an anachronism, and that the particular historical realities the writer must grasp should dictate their own formal conditions.

Nine of Ford's thirty-one published novels are nevertheless historical novels. It was not until *The Good Soldier* that he felt ready to slough off the uncomfortable skin of the historical novel. By that time he had written *Romance* with Conrad; the great *Fifth Queen* trilogy consisting of *The Fifth Queen* (1906), *Privy Seal* (1907), and *The Fifth Queen Crowned* (1908); *The "Half Moon"* (1909), about Henry Hudson's voyage of exploration in 1609; *The Portrait* (1910), placed in the reign of William and Mary; *Ladies Whose Bright Eyes* (1911), juxtaposing the middle ages with the modern world, and *The Young Lovell* (1913), Ford's most beautiful romance, set in the Border country during the reign of Henry VII. As a group, these novels make up a continuous and solid center within Ford's oeuvre—or, to use Professor Smith's metaphor, they are the backbone of Ford's work during his most prolific period as a writer—between 1905 and 1915, the year *The Good Soldier* was published.[1]

Curiously, Ford returned to the historical novel after *Parade's End* (1924–1928): *A Little Less Than Gods* (1928) deals with Napoleon's return from Elba and his subsequent defeat and is concerned with a generation as disillusioned and "lost" as the generation that followed World War I. But it is not quite true to say that Ford returned to the historical novel after *Parade's End*, since his intention was to make that large novel the culmination of his historical fiction—as indeed it is. His statement about *Parade's End* in *It Was the Nightingale* is unequivocal: "I wanted the Novelist in fact to appear in his really proud position as historian of his own time. Proust being dead I could see no one who was doing that. . . ."

Historical fiction as a genre assumes that we tend to see the present in terms of the past. *The Fifth*

Queen—called by Conrad "the swan song of historical romance"—is the story of Katherine Howard, the fifth wife of Henry VIII. Katherine feels herself to be different from Henry's other wives, but her sense of her own individuality cannot save her from her fate, to be merely the fifth in the long procession of Henry's queens. The world of the novel is a world of riddles that the heroine must unravel for herself. As Ford presents the court of Henry VIII, it is an emblem of the modern world at its most complex and unfathomable, with Katherine forced to "read" and interpret events and motives. In this respect the novel strikes the true Fordian note and anticipates the later and better-known novels, *The Good Soldier* and *Parade's End.*

In at least one of his other historical novels, Ford reversed the conventional premise of historical fiction and asked, what if we were to see the past in terms of the present? *Ladies with Bright Eyes* (1911) examines both what is gained and what is lost when the question is translated into a comic collision between two time frames—the early fourteenth century and the early twentieth century—as well as between two kinds of landscape—the inner or subjective and the outer or external. Ford claimed in his dedication to have worked harder on *Ladies* than he had on any of his other novels; certainly it was one of his most popular books and enjoyed several printings, owing its success at least in part to its engaging theme, suggested of course by Mark Twain's Yankee at the court of King Arthur.

Mr. Sorrell, a London publisher, is hurled into the fourteenth century by a train wreck. Finding himself alone on the Salisbury plain "in the middle of the middle ages," he exclaims: "I am not really the chap who belongs to this show." His first spontaneous attempt to interpret what has happened to him is a statement that could speak for the sense of shock and dislocation Ford—and the heroes of all his novels— experienced at finding themselves in the twentieth century. In his exasperation at the course of events, Mr. Sorrell asks: "Have we got to go on playing this old pageant all the time? Can't we let it up just a minute?"—words which look forward to the idea implicit in the title of *Parade's End*.

Ladies plays with an idea that often presents itself to imaginative people: that there is something rather accidental and arbitrary in our being born into a given time and place. (Pound had described Ford as an *halluciné*, one whose real life is elsewhere.) Mr. Sorrell, after surviving the tremendous plunge backward across six centuries, adapts himself so well to his new life that he becomes "a native of the place and time"—an achievement he cannot repeat so easily when he is brought back at the end of the book to the twentieth century, which he hates: "the place is vulgar. The time is vulgar." If he succeeds in becoming once more a native of twentieth-century England, it is only because of the help of Dionissia, the lady with bright eyes (the title of the novel comes from Milton's "L'Allegro"), whose common sense and discipline teach him that he cannot copy the past exactly, as he would like to do, and that one's business in life is "to make a good job of what one's got in hand." The final pages of the novel, in its 1911 version (the ending was changed in 1935), convey "the wisdom of Chaucer and the Bible"—of taking pleasure simply in existing and finding happiness "from day to day."

Ladies is, of course, an idyll and a fantasy, but the questions it raises are serious and real and recurrent in all of Ford's books. What are the attitudes proper toward one's time? Which ideals of an earlier time are to be kept and how? How can we become natives "to the place and time"? What are the alternatives if we fail? What are the possible ways of "moving with the times," as Mr. Sorrell put it?

The nineteenth century was said to have opened with the railroad; Ford opened *Ladies*—and later opened *Parade's End*—with a speeding train that takes each of the protagonists out of the nineteenth century and into an unfamiliar world, where each man must determine his own relationship to the place and time in which he finds himself. As a practical man, Mr. Sorrell goes along with events, fitting himself into them and keeping an open mind, a habit which serves him admirably, for he must sort out for himself at any given moment "what would be an anachronism and what would not."

Ford had, in the same year (1911), written *The Simple Life Limited,* a delightful yet mordant novel about a group of people who very self-consciously adopt what they conceive to be the simple life of the middle ages, translating their collective anachronistic imagination into a way of life that is silly, pretentious, and fraudulent. All of Ford's books, and particularly these two early and explicit fables about the historical imagination, deal with the problems of getting the modern world into focus, of acquiring historical perspective in a quickly changing world, and his constant theme was the need to go back in order to go forward.

The Autobiographical Writing

It has often been pointed out that Ford began the writing of memoirs rather early in life, as if the impulse to look backward asserted itself precociously. The first of the volumes was entitled *Ancient Lights and Certain New Reflections: Being the Memories of a Young Man* (the American edition is entitled *Mem-*

ories and Impressions: A Study in Atmospheres). Written at thirty-seven, it deals with Ford's childhood:

I made for myself the somewhat singular discovery that I can only be said to have grown up a very short time ago. . . . I discovered that I had grown up only when I discovered quite suddenly that I was forgetting my own childhood.

No one has ever given a better reason for writing about his own life. He put his childhood down on paper apparently just in time to rescue it, though it never seemed to be in any real danger of being lost: "To myself I never seemed to have grown up," he tells us later in *Ancient Lights*. If the incidents and personalities of his childhood threatened to dim in adult life, his feelings about himself and the world were continuous with those he had experienced as a child.

I have a vague, but very strong, feeling that everyone else who surrounds me equally has not grown up. They have not in essentials changed since they were small children. . . . The murderer who to-morrow will have the hangman's noose round his neck . . . will feel when the rope is put round his throat, an odd, pained feeling that some mistake is being made, because you do not really hang a child of six in civilized countries.

Ancient Lights was published in 1911, the same year in which Ford published *The Simple Life Limited* and *Ladies*, those novels that examine in different ways the wish to return to the past and what happens when we try. It is as if Ford were stirred by the act of writing his first book of reminiscences to pursue, in as many ways as he could, the meaning of the act of turning back and therefore living simultaneously in two eras. Ten years later, in 1921, came *Thus to Revisit*, his second book of reminiscences—"a sort of continuation of my *Ancient Lights* . . . being concerned

rather with today than yesterday." After another ten
years, *Return to Yesterday*, his third volume, appeared in 1931, covering the period from 1894 to the
outbreak of World War I on August 4, 1914, a date
which marked for Ford the end of the nineteenth century as well as a wrenching of his own life that left
it broken into two parts.

Return to Yesterday was not, however, the title
Ford had wanted: there were eight other titles he
would have preferred (one of them being "Let Us
Now Praise Famous Men"), most of them derived from
and expressing the mood of Ecclesiastes. His American publisher prevailed, however, Ford observing "I
do not think this is a good title for America, but it is
not so bad for England. (80 per cent of Americans
hate to think of Yesterday.) " While the title does not
strike the note Ford intended, which was the remembrance of the past rather than the return to it (Ford
knew that time can not be reversed) , it is clear that
Ford meant *Return to Yesterday* to be paired with the
last of the memoirs, *It Was the Nightingale* (1933) ,
originally called *Towards Tomorrow*. If Ford turned
early and naturally toward the past, it was not for its
own sake but for the sake of the continuity of human
culture; the two impulses—looking back and looking
ahead—were not in conflict but in equipoise. *It Was
the Nightingale*, perhaps his most beautiful and moving book of reminiscences, is a continuation of *Return
to Yesterday*, picking up from 1918 and moving "to
the edge of the abyss of 1929"; but as his last novels
confirm, the abyss can be climbed out of as well as
fallen into.

Categories overlap, and these four volumes are
by no means the only sources of Ford's reminiscences.
The biography of his grandfather Ford Madox Brown
(1896) and the critical books *Dante Gabriel Rossetti*
(1902), *The Pre-Raphaelite Brotherhood* (1907),

Henry James (1913), *Joseph Conrad: A Personal Remembrance* (1924), and *Portraits from Life* (1937) are rich in anecdote and recollection, Ford's own life having been closely connected with the lives of his subjects. In addition, there is the volume of war reminiscences he called *No Enemy* (1929); and there is a good deal of autobiographical detail in his books on culture, where he was as vivid and graphic and illustrative as possible—"to make you see," as he and Conrad used to say about the purpose of the novel.

The dividing line between fiction and autobiography was never a clear one for Ford: the writing of any book, he felt, would be greatly improved by applying to it the canons of the novel. Besides, as he remarked in *It Was the Nightingale*, "novel-writing is a sport infinitely more exciting than the other form." In the dedicatory letter he explained:

I have tried then to write a novel drawing my material from my own literary age. . . . I have employed every wile known to me as novelist—the time-shift, the *progression d'effet*, the adaptation of rhythms to the pace of the action.

And he might have added to his list the art of apparent digression.

Ford had great scorn for writing that was slavishly literal or deficient in design; most of the biographical and autobiographical writing he disliked fell into these categories. What a book about a man's life should not be, he felt, is a mass of detail hung on a mechanically chronological framework. If it is, the writer neither creates a living work nor recreates a living being.

It is important to remember that Ford had an unusually strong sense of privacy, and his autobiographical writings on the whole reinforce it. In the dedicatory letter to *It Was the Nightingale*, he comments on his previous reminiscences—"of which the main features were found in the lives of other people and in which, as well as I could, I obscured myself." But his treatment of his own life is not much more open in *It Was the Nightingale*. In spite of an increased amount of personal material, the novelistic treatment succeeds in distancing it, and the narrator's voice is more like that of a character in a novel than the voice of the author speaking directly to the reader. It may be that Ford's interest in form had as much to do with the idea of biography and autobiography as art rather than sheer documentation as it had to do with his impulse to conceal at the same time he revealed.

Perhaps the most artful, the most difficult, and the least appreciated of his autobiographical works is *No Enemy*, a curious book that resists classification. Labeled sometimes as "disguised autobiography" and sometimes as "disguised fiction," it is best described both as "semifictional war reminiscences" and "a philosophic commentary on the theme of personal survival."[2] Although it is frequently counted among Ford's novels, it is not a novel at all, having no story (in the usual sense) to tell, no characters of whom we could say they have separate existences: there is only a number of Ford's characteristics distributed between the Compiler (or narrator) and the Poet Gringoire, whom the narrator interviews after the war on regular Saturday afternoons, getting down his war reminiscences and reflections; and there is a procession of remembered figures whose significance the mind of the Poet works over in the attempt to heal itself after the suffering of the war.

Ford had started *No Enemy* before the Armistice and finished it by 1920, though it was not published until 1929, Ford regarding it as "too personal to publish at once." It is in fact a very personal—and at the same time objective—account of the process of regaining sanity—"a tale of reconstruction," as its subtitle indicates. And it is a book of great subtlety and self-knowledge, a document of extraordinary psychological interest. Taken as a work of autobiography, it is the most original and introspective book Ford wrote in that apparent genre; at the same time, it is undeniably odd and elusive—yet much more open and less ironic, for all its irony, than his other autobiographical books. It is clearly a book he had to write for himself—something that had to be done, like an account that needed settling, before he could go on to the writing of more novels—the unfinished *True Love and a General Court Martial*, the unpublished *That Same Poor Man* (also called *Mr. Croyd*), *The Marsden Case* (1923), and following it, the books making up *Parade's End*.

No Enemy is, as Ford announced it,

the story of Gringoire just after . . . Armageddon. For it struck the writer that you hear of the men that went, and you hear of what they did when they were There. But you never hear how It left them. You hear how things were destroyed, but seldom of the painful processes of Reconstruction.

The first part of *No Enemy* draws upon the power of particular landscapes, noticed in the course of the war as an artist notices—"for themselves," rather than as "only a background for emotions." Gringoire explains:

. . . Before August, 1914, I lived more through my eyes than through any other sense, and in consequence certain corners of the earth had, singularly, the power to stir me.

But from the moment the war broke out, "aspects of the earth no longer existed for him," with the exception of four—really five—landscapes that became

fixed points, spots of time* for the mind under stress
to repair to, reverting to its most nourishing activity—
storing itself with "observed aspects." These moments
have become part of the poet's "immediate self," and
he explores their meaning, with precision and deli-
cacy and gratitude for their benefactions.

In a general way the book is concerned with how
the sentient mind relates itself to the external world:
how it acts upon and in turn is acted upon by particular stimuli. More specifically, Ford's intention was
to write a book about the nature of the mind under
stress—the particular way it perceives, what it selects
and uses, how it survives: and in the Poet's case how
the mind strengthens itself so that it can again function in a creative way.

No Enemy has a special interest then as a picture
of the writer's mind as it works both under stress and
in tranquility, taking in the fragmented experience of
war, making notes of significant details, seeing con-
nections between them, shaping them, generalizing—
and the mind, always aware of itself, comments on its
own complexity.

Ford uses the word poet in the universal sense of
artist: Gringoire is the poet as novelist:

I have passed twenty-five years of my life in trying to find
new cadences; in chasing assonances out of my prose, with
an enraged meticulousness that might have been that of
Uncle Flaubert himself.

And Ford is careful to make the distinction between
the poet's mind and other minds. For example

---

* The presence of William Wordsworth seems to in-
form the whole book. Its subject (the nature of perception
and reality), its language, its conclusions, suggest the
Wordsworth of *The Prelude,* of "Michael," of "Resolution
and Independence."

. . . The Portsmouth guns of the 28/6/'19 sounding through
the birds' voices from the hill . . . brought it all back. Poets
are like that and have these visions.

Again:

. . . One could hardly look at the gray plains with the
pollard willows marching like aligned candle flames toward the horizon—one avoided looking at it, because it was
Lost Territory, held down, oppressed, as if it were ashamed.
. . . So the poet's mind worked, at leisure, on personal
matters, as neither the mind of Intelligence, or Infantry,
Officer need work.

It was the effort, habitual with Gringoire, to stand
away from his experiences at the same time he lives
through them that saves him from madness and self-
pity. The habit of aloofness permits the Poet's mind
to free itself of its bedevilments long enough to make
patterns of its own experience, dominating rather
than being engulfed by its own suffering. What dis-
tinguishes the Poet is that he can turn his experience
into art; this process, conspiring with the saving
powers of landscape, sees him through the worst of
the war.

In the first part of *No Enemy*, the Poet sees human figures in terms of the landscape. Take, for example, this comparison between French and English
peasants:

North French peasants, slow, ungainly, with heavy legs and
feet. They were just the peasants one had always seen;
hard, like granite—not comparatively gray, like our own
old peasants, who, when they look hard have the aspect not
of wrinkled stone but of old, crannied, oak-tree boles.

The second part of *No Enemy* weaves the memory of
particular men and women with that of "certain in-
teriors"—and running through the whole of the book
is the idea of the unity of nature and human life and
the life human beings create—whether they perceive

nature through a seeing eye or whether they build houses and cities or write books.

Some of Ford's best writing is to be found in *No Enemy*, and there are arresting passages whose beauty seems to derive from his intuition of the connection between men and things, and from his sense that the universe is intensely alive—even when it is most vulnerable. Describing himself as a "creature of dreads," Ford projects that state of mind on to the houses, even the curtains of ruined houses. Take these two passages:

. . . Ever since he had been a tiny child . . . he had, he said, been so much a creature of dreads that this was, in a sense, much less than dreads to which he had been well accustomed. The dreads of original sin, of poverty, of bankruptcy, of incredible shyness, of insults, misunderstandings, of disease, of death, of succumbing to blackmailers, forgers, brain-troubles, punishments, undeserved ingratitudes, betrayals.—There was nothing, Gringoire said, that he hadn't dreaded in a sufficiently long life "which had been, mostly, a matter of one dread knocking out another."

and

Just as trees and fields appeared to dread the contamination of alien presences, so with buildings. Only with buildings—and more particularly with houses—the feeling was very much enhanced. They seemed to dread not only contaminations, but pains, violations, physical shames, and dissolution in fire.

—or his description of Pont de Nieppe, near Armentières:

I remember that what struck me most . . . was still the feeling of abashment that seemed to attach to furniture and wall-paper exposed to the sky . . . what struck me as infinitely pathetic was lace curtains: for there were innumerable lace curtains, that had shaded vanished windows, fluttering from all the unroofed walls in the glassless window-frames. They seemed to me to be more forlornly ashamed than any human beings I have ever seen. Only brute beasts ever approach that: old and weary horses, in nettle-grown fields; or dogs when they go away into bushes to die.

Among the figures Gringoire recalls in the second part, the young sculptor Henri Gaudier-Brzeska, killed in the war in 1915, had for him a kind of divinity:

There, he seemed as if he stood amidst sunlight; as if indeed he floated in a ray of sunlight, like the dove in Early Italian pictures. In a life during which I have known thousands of people; thousands and thousands of people; during which I have grown sick and tired of "people" so that I prefer the society of cabbages, goats, and the flowers of the marrow plant; I have never otherwise known what it was to witness an appearance which symbolized so completely—aloofness. It was like the appearance of Apollo at a creditors' meeting. It was supernatural.

Gaudier was the type of the artist—"so entirely inspired by inward visions . . . as if his eyes were fixed on a point within himself. . . ."

And Gringoire recalls Rosalie Prudent, whom he came upon in an evacuated town, making an evacuated house her own, sewing in the twilight, with the Germans shelling the church nearby—"so oblivious to the very real danger, so brave and so tranquil."

Mme. Rosalie sewed as if she had no other pride and no other purpose in the world. For she told of the fate of her men and her womenfolk abstractedly and passionlessly; pride only showed itself when she talked of the state of the house in which she had found a refuge. From time to time she would say that if Mm. the Proprietors returned, they would find the floors waxed; the stair-rods shining, the windows polished. . . . That was her pride. . . .

Gaudier and Mme. Rosalie are among the figures who serve as paradigms for the Poet—figures from whom Gringoire could draw the strength to persevere

—"to dig myself in." They are embodiments of "the doctrine of pride in work as work; of engrossment and serenity; of aloofness from the world and of introspection with no other purpose. . . . I see no other lesson in life."

Digging in, as Gringoire tells us, is the lesson of the war, if any lesson is to be learned at all. It has taught him "what a hell—what a hell!—of a lot we can do without." It has taught him to simplify, pare down, fall back on his essential self, which must be self-sufficient so that it can give to as well as take from the world. The entire latter part of *No Enemy* points toward the arguments of *Provence* and *Great Trade Route,* arguments offered in the 1930s in the hope of averting another world war.

The title of *No Enemy* refers, of course, to the song in *As You Like It,* to the lines "Here shall he see/ No enemy/ But winter and rough weather." "Under the greenwood tree" is an invitation to perfect repose or "sanctuary," as Ford called it. What he meant was something inviolable and curative, a place where the "long strain" and the "dreads" could be lifted. "We must have in the world assured nooks and houses," he wrote: that is, "no enemy but winter and rough weather." To have only the natural problems of life seemed idyll enough after the war.

The Books on Culture

Ford was primarily a novelist, but a large part of his published work took the form of discussions of culture, books that can be read either for their own sake or for the sake of the novels. Either way they deserve more serious attention than they have been given. Like the novels—and the books of reminiscence —these critical books express a way of looking at human culture that is consistent and coherent and that suggests possible directions now—perhaps even more compellingly than when Ford first offered them.

Ford had an abiding belief in the wholeness of human life and in the possibilities of restoring life to wholeness in spite of the disintegrative forces of modern life. It would hardly be overstating to say that he had a vision of unity, and that it informed all his work, giving to each part a characteristic largeness of perspective.

His books of cultural criticism took the form of studies of particular places: his concern was to render their atmospheres, allowing each place to reveal its particular character and pursuing the implications of each trait—with the extreme caution, as he once put it, of the novelist. The books seem to fall naturally into several groups.

First, the early books on England. In 1900 he wrote *The Cinque Ports: A Historical and Descriptive Record*, followed by three books on English life: *The Soul of London: A Survey of a Modern City* (1905), *The Heart of the Country: A Survey of a Modern Land* (1906), and *The Spirit of the People: An Analysis of the English Mind* (1907). In addition, an essay "The Future of London" appeared in 1909.

Ford wrote two books of anti-German propaganda during the war—*When Blood Is Their Argument: An Analysis of Prussian Culture* (1915) and *Between St. Dennis and St. George: A Sketch of Three Civilizations* (English, French, and German, 1915).

Between the two world wars he published *A Mirror to France* (1926), the two overlapping *New York Essays* (1927) and *New York Is Not America: Being a Mirror to the States* (1927); and finally the two large-scale discussions on what Mediterranean culture had to offer to a world intent on the next war, *Provence* (1935) and *Great Trade Route* (1937).

The Cinque Ports (1900) is a history and appreciation of the five towns in Kent and Sussex—Hastings, Romney, Hythe, Dover, and Sandwich—that, together with Winchelsea and Rye, had a singular role in English history as a "kingdom within a kingdom," a little group of commonwealths granted autonomy by the English government in exchange for providing a stipulated number of ships for England's defense. Ford knew the towns well, having lived in one or another of them when he was younger; he loved them and was fascinated by their history— haunted by it, as he said—as well as by their character.

To write *The Cinque Ports*, he did the work of an archival historian, reading the available documents; what he produced was a book of great freshness and grace and fluidity, striking the note he was to sustain in what became a distinctively Fordian mode—a mixture of history, personal commentary, and "sociological impressionism." As he pointed out in his dedicatory letter, the book was to be "neither archaeological nor topographical, nor even archaeologico-topographical. It was to be a piece of literature pure and simple, an attempt, by means of suggestion, to interpret to the passing years the inward message of the Cinque Ports." Perhaps it was the intersection of the historian's and the novelist's imagination that gave the genre, as Ford used it, its special quality.

Writing for an age that would, he feared, want to have less and less to do with the study of history, Ford wrote as chronicler of something fine and vanished and deserving to be remembered—a civilization based on ideals of craftsmanship and independence. But in *The Cinque Ports*, he keeps firmly before the reader a double image of the past and present, each commenting on the other; and he locates conflicting values in the course of the rise and fall of this civilization, which he takes as a microcosm of the larger world. He notes, for example, the "obtuseness of municipalities," when the Winchelsea burghers were "so intent upon the preservation of the land which the receding sea gave them, that they forgot that the sea's recessional was the death-hymn of the town's greatness," its economy being based on its function as a port.

And in his essay "The Future of London" (1909), which appeared as a chapter in *London Town Past and Present* by W. W. Hutchings, Ford speaks of the tyranny of the future and the tyranny of the past.

The Future has only the idealism of a dim and unbefriended reason to wage war with. The Past uses this idealism of the picturesque, the Ancient, the Faith of our Fathers. It arms itself with the weapons of pathos, of habit, of want of imagination, and of an irrational reason.

Ford writes so that his own generation will not be "the tyrants of the men to come." A "city consciousness" must be awakened to prevent "catastrophes." "If for want of vigilance we let beautiful places be defiled, it is they [our children] who will find it a hopeless task to restore them." City planning must reckon with the "stealthy figure of the speculative builder": Ford wisely divides the future into the Future Probable and the Future Utopian in his discussion of urban planning. He urges "controlled growth-planning" to avoid "a scarlet fever, a pimply rash of suburban . . . villas." "The city itself," he wrote, "must take hold of what grows around it." All this in 1909.

The titles of his books on England use what was even when he wrote them an old-fashioned vocabulary. In a century that was to be dominated by technology, as he saw clearly in 1905, he insisted that nations and cities have souls, hearts, and spirits, are a collective living organism. *The Soul of London* is a highly poetic and subjective response to the experience of the modern city ("the modern spirit" expressing itself "in terms not of men but of forces," in "great organizations run by men as impersonal as the atoms of our own frames").

Ford's own impulse as a poet—hardly subterranean, for he published a dozen volumes of poetry in the course of his life—his poet's eye for image and detail, his rhythms, were nevertheless absorbed by— were responsible for—his best prose. *The Soul of London* can be read partly as early sociology, with no pretense at scientific method (a fact which does not make the study less accurate), partly as a prose poem, an early contribution in prose to the poetry of the modern city. Published twelve years before T. S. Eliot's "The Love Song of J. Alfred Prufrock," *The Soul of London* signals the ways in which poetry could, in the twentieth century, derive its energy from the sense of the diminution of life lived in the city. Ford noted the characteristic material out of which poets would make their poetry: "the grimy upper windows through which appear white faces," "certain corners of streets, certain angles of buildings . . . odours, familiar sounds."

A man may look down out of dim windows upon the slaty, black, wet misery of a squalid street, upon a solitary flickering lamp that wavers a sooty light upon a solitary, hurrying passer's umbrella. . . . A sudden consonance with his mood . . . a sudden significance will be there in the bleak wet street. . . .

Approaching London by train, Ford looks through the window:

One is behind glass as if one were gazing into the hush of a museum; one hears no street cries, no children's call. . . . One sees . . . so many little bits of uncompleted life. . . . I looked down upon black and tiny yards that were like the cells in an electric battery.

The Heart of the Country, dedicated to Henry James, is "a rendering of rural cosmogony" worthy of the master in its accuracy and knowledge of the life rendered. The first chapter, "Between the Hedgerows," defines "the country":

Land, in fact, that has any very distinctive features—moors, hills, peaks, downs, marshes, or fens—such land is not the country. It is only where the hedgerows journey beside the turnpikes, close in the sunken lanes, or from a height are seen, like the meshes of an ill-made net, to lie lightly upon hills and dales, to parcel off irregular squares of vivid green from jagged rhomboids of brown, of yellow, or of purple— it is only where the hedgerow has its agricultural use that the country of the townsman is. . . . Always the hedgerow shuts in the horizon, so that to go into the country is, as it were, to lose oneself in a maze; whereas to go, say, on to Lobden moorside, is to expose oneself nakedly to the skies.

Ford's understanding of topography was matched by his knowledge of the lives of the country men and women both as individuals (he loved them for their "strong individualities") and as members of a class— the tramps, the paupers, the wagoners, the peasants, the large landowners and the small.

"Ah keep all on gooing!": Ford liked to quote Meary Walker, a poor old peasant woman he had known in Kent, and his account of her obscure life appears in two other books of his.[3] For him, her life was a model of fortitude: she was an ordinary human being transcending ordinariness by force of her character, becoming a fixed moral and psychological point of reference for him. (Later he would write: "So I keep on writing," echoing his Meary's simple determination; her image helped him through depression, illness, and poverty, to make new beginnings.)

Ford's early study of Englishness, *The Spirit of the People*, can be taken as a gloss on the novels: the chapter on conduct has *The Good Soldier* already in its bones. Read carefully, the book shows a balanced understanding of the English gentleman's code of behavior that should lay to rest all the talk about Ford's romantic illusions. On the one hand:

. . . The especial province of the English nation is the evolution of a standard of manners. . . . The province of the Englishman is to solve the problem of how men may live together.

On the other hand:

To the attaining of this standard the Englishman has sacrificed the arts—which are concerned with the expression of emotions—and his knowledge of life, which cannot be attained to by a man who sees the world as all good. . . .

The Englishman's naïveté about the world and his "want of imagination" are matched by his ignorance of his own feelings and his inarticulateness about them. The general English tendency toward self-repression Ford found less and less admirable; by the time he was ready to write *Parade's End*, he "had arrived," as he tells us in *It Was the Nightingale*, "at the stage of finding the gentleman an insupportable phenomenon." But before he had done with the theme, Ford was to use the Englishman's (his own!) fear of a scene as the material of some of his best scenes.

His distinction between English Catholicism and English Protestantism is especially useful for readers of the novels, explaining an area that is often puzzling:

Speaking very broadly, we may say that Catholicism, which is a religion of action and of frames of mind, is a religion that men can live up to. Protestantism no man can live up to, since it is a religion of ideals and of reason. (I am far from wishing to adumbrate to which religion I give my preference; for I think it will remain to the end a matter for dispute whether a practicable or an ideal code be the more beneficial to humanity) . . . . The [Puritan] Revolution doomed England to be the land of impracticable ideals. Before that date a man could live without his finger upon his moral pulse. . . .

Ford wrote two books on German culture at the request of his friend C. F. G. Masterman, a member of Asquith's cabinet (Asquith was British prime minister from 1908 to 1916) and director of the British Ministry of Information during the war. As Allied propaganda, *When Blood Is Their Argument* and *Between St. Dennis and St. George* were all that was expected of them. The latter book was published in French as well as English and read widely in France, and Ford was formally commended for it by the French Minister of Instruction. But the books interest us now because they express a passionate set of convictions about many of the issues our century is still reckoning with.

Ford's attack on the German university system is central to his argument. "All my life I have been fighting German scholarship," he wrote. The Prussian educational machine as an instrument of Prussian nationalism and militarism had "reduced all learning, all criticism, and all philosophy, which implies the judgment of life, to . . . Philologie," which Ford saw as a narrow and mechanical pedantry enjoining "an extremely minute and industrious attention . . . to every possible department of fact connected with the work"—except its spirit.

German philology was merely "a form of industry like another," calling "for no special gifts" and becoming dangerous because it "began to take the place of learning, which is a thing open only to those temperamentally equipped for appreciation of one art or another." Prussian "factual meticulousness" was "like the hunger of wolves"; it spelled the death of the arts and of the historic sense.

The real object of the German university was "the training of correct state officials by correct state officials" and produced a way of thinking that was antagonistic alike to the idea of individuality and to the open and free examination of ideas—hence the German habit of worshiping a great figure (a habit that Hitler was to exploit). "Essentially the way of the sword has been the way of Prussia"; the study of German philology has been "always a process of discovering new arguments for the way of the sword." The German university was making "a technology of humanistic learning" in order "to turn out monomaniacs" instead of reasonable human beings. The end of education should be to broaden the mind; Prussian education narrowed it to make it fit for one kind of specialization or another, all of which in the end would serve to feed a great war machine.

It was not that Ford failed to appreciate thoroughness; craftsmanship meant everything to him, and the sense of honor that is the mark of the heroes of his novels is essentially a love of detail. But to be so lost in detail that the gaze is rigid and cannot take in the whole meant being—as he liked to say—"without knowledge of life." In the choice between "professionalization or amateurism in politics, the arts, the universities, and every department of life," Ford was on the side of the amateur, the man with a broader and more balanced point of view.

There are, of course, two great educational theories in the world—the one, which I will roughly call the German theory—careers, professions, trades. The other to awaken the sense of general observation and to develop all-round qualities in a man who will afterwards specialize. The practical upshot of the matter is at the moment of writing being tried out upon the fields of Flanders.

Rebecca West had reviewed *Between St. Dennis and St. George* when it appeared in 1915; she opened with a delighted complaint:

It is really not quite fair that a man who spends his whole existence in the consideration of beauty, the values of life, and the niceties of language, should be able to stroll out of his garden, look on for a minute at the fight of the controversialists in the highway, and say the right, the illuminating, the decisive thing that settles the whole affair, and leaves them sitting, hot and silly, in the dust.[4]

"One is surprised," she concluded, ". . . that an artist can make so fine a controversialist; but as one reads . . . one wonders how any but an artist can ever be a controversialist"—a conclusion that supports Ford's trust in the flexibility of an educated mind.

It was precisely from his point of view as an artist that Ford offered, in the late 1930s, his criticism of modern life—"our makeshift for a civilization"—in *Provence* and *Great Trade Route*: "I am neither sociologist nor politician. I am an onlooker stating the result of conclusions that have taken me half a century to arrive at." An observer of life: his late books tended to be panoramic—long sweeping views of life and art (*Provence, Great Trade Route,* the uncompleted *A History of Our Own Times* projected in three volumes, *The English Novel, The March of Literature*). His conclusions, sensible enough (those of a "depressed optimist," he said), were that "the world is dying"—not dead but dying—and that it was still possible to rebuild it, provided we had an idea of how to go about it.

Do you happen to know Haydn's symphony? . . . It is a piece that begins with a full orchestra, each player having beside him a candle to light his score. They play that delicate cheerful-regretful music of an eighteenth-century that was already certain of its doom. . . . As they play on the contrabassist takes his candle and on tiptoe steals out of the orchestra; then the flautist takes his candle and steals away. . . . The music goes on—and the drum is gone, and the bassoon . . . and the hautbois, and the second . . . violin. . . . Then they are all gone and it is dark. . . . That is our age.

And Ford offers us the frame of mind of the culture of Provence as an alternative to our own.

Provence is, of course, a real place, and Ford spent many years of his life there. "If I write a sentence [in London] it comes out as backboneless as a water hose. . . . When I get back to Provence . . . I shall write little crisp sentences like silver fish jumping out of streams." It was the place in which he lived for almost all his spiritual life, as he put it, his first sight of it having been the "most memorable sensation of my life."

It is as if one wakened from a dream of immortality to the realisation of what is earthly permanence. And, ever since I first had that sensation in a train hastening through the dawn I have had two existences—a Provence life that was persistent and a life of other regions on the Great Route that were forever changing.

Provence was then a state of mind as well as a real place, and it became for Ford an idea of perfection in art and in life, something like Yeats's Byzantium—a region where the soul can live, a "blessed oasis," Ford called it, "in the insupportable madhouse for apes that is our civilization." Provence was his image of the golden age, an image not of precivilization but of civilization at its best, "the loveliness" and "the gladness" that "civilization should be."

For his argument, Ford elaborated the image of the Great Trade Route, the ancient highway nourish-

ing a great civilization and along which "travelled
continually the stream of the arts, of thought, of the
traditions of life." Beginning in China, "where they
made beautiful, intricate, and improbable stuffs," the
immense caravans of the merchants of the Route "set
out, whole holy cities at a time, to spread the sweet-
ness of herbs, the softness of silks and ritual and cults
and the arts of lacquering and the dance, before al-
tars." From eastern Asia through the Middle East to
Greece and Italy and France and England, the merchants "passed lifetimes passing backwards and for-
wards" along the great oval swathe formed by the
route.

Where they went they left civilizations—the ancient civilizations of the resounding and romantic names—Samarkand
and Ispahan and Trebizond and Damascus and Venice and
Paris and Tintagel. And their traces remain forever, since
it is to them that we owe our arts, our cults, our thought,
and what is left to us of the love of peace and sunshine. . . .

It is all very far from the monolithic, technologi-
cal, militaristic world Ford was contemplating in the
1930s, too late, but perhaps just in time, to announce
his theme:

If you could get rid of wars, national barriers, patriotisms,
politicians, and written constitutions, you might, at the
hands of the Small Producer, experience a return to a real
Golden Age.

In politics he described himself sometimes as a
radical, sometimes as a quietist anarchist: do away
with nations and professional politicians; decentralize
and keep only neighborhoods that will run themselves
—advice that seems less startling in the 1970s than it
did when Ford was giving it. "Patriotism is the mean-
est of virtues," one which "the gods who wish to destroy our civilization invented to drive us mad." In
short, an exchange "of civilizations, not bombs": "all

we people on the Great Trade Route are one civilisa-
tion."

Behind Ford's idea of small political units and
a horticultural economy of small producers engaged
in market-gardening was his strong feeling for the
sacredness of the concrete and a distrust of the abstractions of science and technology. "Men cannot exist
with mass-production and remain men." An economy
based on mass-production "and the worship of mass-
production" makes the machine the master rather
than the servant of men; the individual must regain
mastery over his own life. "Like the Giant Antaeus
. . . our civilization needs contact with the earth for
its renewal." Men and women can lead simpler and
better lives if they get back to, rather than move still
further away from, the sources of their lives.

The prospects for the future of the race occupied
him a good deal: "The real danger ahead is the food
danger." And in his anxieties about overpopulation
and insufficient food (as well as adulterated and syn-
thetic food, which he detested), about the damage
done to nature by industrialized society and the squan-
dering of the earth's resources by a consumer economy,
he saw very far ahead.

Ford really believed that a change in the public
heart—and the individual heart—could save the
world. The "non-machine" society of small producers,
devoted to the growing of green plants and practicing
the virtue of frugality, is an expanded metaphor,
worked out along economic lines, for his moral ideas
about what the self should be—self-sustaining and au-
tonomous, able not only to survive but to regenerate
itself.

The subjects of *Great Trade Route* are, as Ford
announced at the beginning, "two heroes and one
heroine." He was referring to the chief ideas he was

to treat, and in fact he treated them as if they were characters in a novel. "Let your generous sympathies go with the loser," he advised, and in his book the exploited peoples of the world take on the aspect of Fordian heroes. Much in advance of his time, he saw the American Indian from the Indian point of view, and the exploitation of Africa was only one more example of the "stealing-a-million-isn't-piracy-psychology" of capitalism. (An observation on slavery suggests a line of approach to the psychology of racial hatred: the abhorrence we feel that one human being should be the property of another "is a natural abhorrence such as all created beings feel for the excrement of their species.")

Provence and *Great Trade Route* are full of much excellent and miscellaneous information—on cooking, on architecture, on Ford's travels in America—all artfully pulled together (the function of digression is, he declared, to refresh the mind) and unified in a celebration of the unity of civilization. The charm and originality of these late books do not detract from their seriousness: art is to be enjoyed, and a consideration of human survival should all the more appropriately take the form of a dance. "*Saltavit. Placuit. Mortuus est.*" ("He danced. He gave pleasure. He is dead.") The memorial tablet of a Roman boy dancer who had died young is the subject of one of Janice Biala's drawings in *Provence*, and the Latin epitaph provides one of the themes running through Ford's last novels. The boy typified an idea of life to which Ford hoped the world would return. His last novels— *When the Wicked Man* (1931), *The Rash Act* (the rash act being suicide, 1933) and its sequel *Henry for Hugh* (1934), and *Vive le Roy* (1936)—are to be read as fantasies about dying and being born again, coming back to a living life. Puzzling and on the whole disregarded, these novels gain in clarity and sense if they are read in the spirit of *Provence* and *Great Trade Route*, their stories allegories of metamorphosis, of the possibilities of self-renewal.

4

The Good Soldier

The Good Soldier, as its readers know from Ford's
dedicatory letter to Stella Bowen in 1927, was Ford's
"great auk's egg," proof to himself and to the world
that if he put everything he knew about the art of
the novel into one book, it would be the book that
would represent him more honorably and accurately
than anything he had ever done. *The Good Soldier*
represented not so much a delayed flowering—Ford
tells us that he started it on his fortieth birthday—as
a working through of complex problems that, under a
new impulse, reached a simultaneous resolution. It
was to be a concentrated, small, perfect version of his
"one" novel: "I fully intended it to be my last book."
And by forcing all that he knew into so small a book,
Ford gained an expressive power he had never before
achieved. It contained all the significant elements of
his work, all that he had learned from writing different kinds of novels—historical novels, romances, novels of contemporary life. It was a crystallization: Ford
had at last found the vocabulary he had been search-
ing for and the absolutely right form for his subject;
at last subject and form could merge perfectly. What
came together miraculously was a novel that has been
widely recognized as a landmark in modern literature,
"like Joyce's *Ulysses* or T. S. Eliot's 'The Waste Land'
. . . defining possibilities and tendencies in the art of

its time and posing basic questions for every new reader concerning the nature of fiction."[1]

The Good Soldier is the story of two couples, the English Ashburnhams and the American Dowells, who meet year after year at a German spa and, on the surface, are friends, just as, on the surface, each couple appears to be married happily enough. In reality—and the action of the novel constantly emphasizes the contrast between appearance and reality—the four figures are connected to one another by the most ambivalent passions, sometimes concealed from the others, sometimes concealed from themselves.

The action is further complicated when Edward Ashburnham falls in love with his ward, Nancy Rufford, and realizes that his passion for her is much more real and more serious than the sentimental affairs he has had—with his wife Leonora's approval and even contrivance—in order to escape the lovelessness of their marriage. Florence Dowell, the wife of the narrator, has been Edward's mistress. When she learns of Edward's love for Nancy, in a paroxysm of jealousy and self-hatred, she commits suicide. Edward kills himself because the alternative—to seduce Nancy—is unthinkable, given the kind of man he is (a good soldier, committed to a sense of honor and duty) ; and Nancy goes mad. Her enigmatic word "shuttlecocks" seems to sum up so much of the feeling of the book: that human beings are in the control of forces they cannot understand.

The narrator of the story, John Dowell (and one of the two husbands) , presents these complications to us, compounding them by unfolding the story not in chronological order, but in the order that his understanding of the events and motives and characters dictates. Dowell's narration seems to be a burrowing into this tangle of relationships, a search for truth. But insofar as Dowell himself is one of the characters involved in the story and hardly disengaged enough for the pursuit of truth, much of his narrative is a justification of his own part. The search for truth becomes even more burdened because Dowell, faced with the breakdown of all the human relationships making up his world—betrayal, madness, suicide—is aware of a parallel disintegration in the larger world: the outbreak of the world war. And he tries to understand the connection between his story and the universal cataclysm.

You may well ask why I write. And yet my reasons are quite many. For it is not unusual in human beings who have witnessed the sack of a city or the falling to pieces of a people to desire to set down what they have witnessed. . . . Someone has said that the death of a mouse from cancer is the whole sack of Rome by the Goths, and I swear to you that the breaking up of our little four-square coterie was such another unthinkable event.

The subject then of *The Good Soldier* is the fall of a civilization and the consequent necessity that the narrator feels to make some sense of what has happened and why—to extract some kind of meaning from the general cataclysm and to speculate about the very nature of civilization and its value.

In understanding the action he has survived to narrate, Dowell raises fundamental questions that are everywhere implicit in the story. Why do men find it impossible to be happy? How can they live if they are not to deny their instincts? What, in that case, are they to do with their instincts? What are they to do with the demands that civilization makes of them and the ways it codifies those demands and regulates human relationships? Given the nature of their natures, how can men work out ways of dealing with the world outside them—and the world they make? How much do men gain from civilization, and what in turn must they give up for it? What is civilization worth—how much suffering? In short, how can men find a workable relationship between their instincts and civilized life?

These questions are so pressing in *The Good Soldier* that Dowell's narration is in large part an attempt to answer them. Freud was to discuss these same questions in two great essays, *Civilization and Its Discontents* and *Beyond the Pleasure Principle*, but it is important to remember that *The Good Soldier* was published fifteen years before the first essay and five years before the second. With great originality, Ford explored novelistically what Freud presented as argument. Ford's novel and Freud's essays strikingly illuminate one another.

━ Ford criticism has by and large arranged itself on either side of the question: how much does the narrator of *The Good Soldier* know? We shall start with the assumption that Dowell knows everything—that is, he knows all the "facts" of the story. He knows what has happened, and he knows his part in all of it; what he does not know is how to interpret any of it; and it is his search for meaning that in turn makes sense of and justifies his extraordinary bedevilment of the reader—that is, Dowell's search for meaning justifies Ford's extraordinary technical achievement in creating Dowell and telling the story through him as he does.

Dowell is a *faux-naif* of the most artful kind, a pretender to innocence, a master of obfuscation, a manipulator of every trick, the most unreliable of unreliable narrators. There are overstatements, understatements, denials, lies, evasions, contradictions, accusations, exaggerations, puns, apparent irrelevancies, logical fallacies, omitted links, digressions, sharp anticipations, delayed explanations, swings of mood, and explosions great and small. He embarrasses, bullies, confuses, and tests the reader; he presumes on his credulity; he cloys, simpers, condescends; he writes of "monstrous things" in a "frivolous manner." He spirals up and down, toward and away from his point, buries it, conceals it, flattens and misleads with false emphasis; he lurches from self-denigration to self-promotion and back; he suddenly varies the intensities and the volume and pushes himself into the story. And he repeats.

The reader must always assume that Dowell knows more than he claims to know about motives and events (and himself); otherwise the story is reduced to a *tour de force*, a stunt, a prodigious display of technique for its own sake, removed from the essential seriousness of its purpose. The book was intended, of course, as a portrayal of the prewar British world, and it is that. But more importantly, it is a setting forth of human relationships in a state of civilization by someone involved in and seriously injured by them, yet intent on understanding the pattern of events.

Dowell's amazing bag of tricks is a complete rhetoric, a strategy that he uses against the reader, so that we are forced to accept the primacy of his existence as narrator rather than as cuckold, eunuch, fool. His hatred for Florence, for Edward, for Leonora, for civilization, for himself—all this he turns toward the reader; and the cruelty—in a book dealing largely with the infliction of pain—and passion, which could find no outlet during his life as Florence's husband, find their outlet through the narration. Through the act of telling, the narrator achieves the potency and effectiveness he has yearned for as Florence's husband and Leonora's confidant. Dowell is bent on vindicating his manliness—and at the same time his sexual purity: "I will vouch for the cleanness of my thoughts and the absolute chastity of my life."

Early in the story he creates a setting in which he places the reader and himself:

So I shall just imagine myself for a fortnight or so at one side of the fireplace of a country cottage, with a sympathetic soul opposite me. And I shall go on talking, in a low voice while the sea sounds in the distance and overhead the great black flood of wind polishes the bright stars.

Dowell, who has been everybody's confidant, has changed places with the reader. He has listened and pieced together for thirteen years, and now it is the reader's turn. The book is insistent on the need to talk, on the very activity of talking: Edward hears the voices of Leonora and Nancy through the wall all through the night ("they lay down in the same bed, talking and talking, all through the night"), and Edward talks to Dowell all through another night. We are prepared to understand Dowell's sense of relief in having the reader to himself. The scene is a realization of what he has wished for: the reader is captive, a "silent listener," and the scene is a fulfillment of Dowell's fantasy, because he has found a means of exchanging roles with the reader. Nursemaid to Florence at the beginning of the action, nursemaid to Nancy at the end, his life is circumscribed by a role he half-wants, half-detests; correspondingly, he gives us two flanking pictures of the reader in attendance on the narrator, the first at the beginning, the second in the last part of the book: "I have stuck to my idea of being in a country cottage with a silent listener, hearing between the gusts of the wind and amidst the noises of the distant sea the story as it comes." The correspondence between life and the narrator's art is precise: in each there are only fragments and glimpses, and the silent listener, the passive reader, must, as the passive Dowell has already done, make an unprecedented effort to see the action as a whole.

We must assume an unrelievedly critical attitude toward everything he tells us and keep our eye on him at every moment, or the story gets away from us.

Should we question *every* statement he gives us or
only some—or most? The diabolism of Ford's narrative method teases us toward the possibility of a reading in which *all* of Dowell's statements must be
questioned and interpreted. The story makes sense
only if we sift and sift for ourselves.

For example, Dowell's readiness to believe in
Florence's pretended heart condition allows him to
keep his wife on the Continent, presumably to save
her life, for the Channel crossing would kill her, as
he knows he is supposed to think. Her doctors (Dowell suspects them of profiting from collusion with
Florence) have told him so. But he keeps her there
really to thwart her ambitions in England and hold
her to a lover she is sick of, so that he, Dowell, can
continue to be the secret spectator of the debasing
affair and continue to judge it. So we know that he
has known all along about Jimmy and Florence and
that, of the two versions of what was happening, he
has endorsed the official version—Florence's and the
doctors'—of her "heart" because it gives him the
means to punish her, enjoy himself, and exercise his
spite.

Again, Dowell offers us two alternative and apparently unrelated explanations for the "heart": one,
that it is a plot hatched by Jimmy and Florence for
the sake of their privacy; the other, that it is Florence's
fear of her husband's capacity for physical violence,
as he demonstrates it to his servant when he drops the
suitcase containing her drugs.

It affirmed in her the desperate resolve to conceal from me
the fact that she was not what she would have called "a pure
woman." For that was really the mainspring of her fantastic
actions. She was afraid that I should murder her. . . .

So she got up the heart attack, at the earliest possible
opportunity, on board the liner.

The reader must choose between two stories that reflect opposing images of the narrator: deceived husband and gull versus angered and dangerous male; that is, between his sexual innocence and his sexual power. We are drawn into the story to make decisions and judgments that the narrator refuses to make directly; we must judge his judgments or we lose the thread.

His periodic claims to nothingness—being nothing, doing nothing, knowing nothing, feeling nothing, thinking nothing, believing nothing—and the pervasive nihilism of his attitudes are a camouflage for his shrinking from conclusions, his fear of experience and his failure to deal with it. They are also a camouflage for repeated, vengeful, and deviously made judgments, even on himself.

But upon my word, I don't know how we put in our time. How does one put in one's time? How is it possible to have achieved nine years and to have nothing whatever to show for it? Nothing whatever, you understand. . . . And, as for experience, as for knowledge of one's fellow beings— nothing either. . . . The instances of honesty that one comes across in this world are just as amazing as the instances of dishonesty. After forty-five years of mixing with one's kind, one ought to have acquired the habit of being able to know something about one's fellow beings. But one doesn't.

And though he often "blames" the English for hiding the abyss under the surface of life, he deeply admires Edward for his style, among other things. In fact, he is jealous of it. In a final comparison, in the last paragraph of the novel, he shows himself, to his own discredit, "trotting" off to Leonora with Nancy's telegram, refraining even from "God bless you" to Edward because it would "not be quite English good form," and allowing Edward to kill himself. Dowell's contempt for himself in this final passage is the least

ambiguous of his judgments, and we accept it as ultimate because of its position.

Dowell "blames" civilization for his own failures
and his refusal to see what is before his eyes. He tells
us at first (in the long passage quoted above) how
impossible it is to acquire any knowledge of human
beings "after forty-five years of mixing with one's
kind." Then, in a characteristic reversal, he assures
us of his expertise, his qualifications for judging: "I
have observed this matter long enough. . . ." Isolated
even from the other three figures in his "minuet," *has*
he mixed with his kind? Is there anyone else in the
world enough like him to be considered his kind?
What does he mean by "one's kind"? What is his evidence worth? Is he implying ironically that by virtue
of being able to discriminate at all between instances
of honesty and dishonesty he is therefore more honest
than, say, his wife?

We watch him through changes of focus and
mood and tone as he saturates himself with rational-
izations and evasions and conventional sentiment until
he reaches an outburst that, though it is as direct a
statement as he is capable of, still needs interpretation.
The whole passage is worth looking at. It is a fine
example of Ford's narrative power.

For, all that time, I was just a male sick nurse. And what
chance had I against those three hardened gamblers [Flor-
ence. Edward, and Leonora], who were all in league to
conceal their hands from me? What earthly chance? They
were three to one—and they made me happy. Oh, God,
they made me so happy that I doubt if even paradise, that
shall smooth out all temporal wrongs, shall ever give me
the like. And what could they have done better, or what
could they have done that could have been worse? I don't
know. . . .

I suppose that, during all that time, I was a deceived
husband and that Leonora was pimping for Edward.

You ask how it feels to be a deceived husband. Just

heavens, I do not know. It feels just nothing at all. It is
not hell, certainly it is not necessarily heaven. So I suppose
it is the intermediate stage. What do they call it? Limbo.
No, I feel nothing at all about that. They [Florence and
Edward] are dead; they have gone before their Judge, who,
I hope, will open to them the springs of His compassion.
. . . But what were they? The just? The unjust? God knows!
I think that the pair of them were only poor wretches
creeping over this earth in the shadow of an eternal wrath.
It is very terrible. . . .

It is almost too terrible, the picture of that judgment,
as it appears to me sometimes, at nights . . . upon an immense plain, suspended in mid-air. I seem to see three
figures, two of them clasped in an intense embrace, and
one intolerably solitary. It is in black and white, my picture
of that judgment, an etching perhaps; only I cannot tell an
etching from a photographic reproduction. And the immense plain is the hand of God, stretching out for miles
and miles, with great spaces above it and below it. And
they are in the sight of God, and it is Florence that is
alone. . . .

And, do you know, at the thought of that intense soli-
tude I feel an overwhelming desire to rush forward and
comfort her. You cannot, you see, have acted as nurse to a
person for twelve years without wishing to go on nursing
her, even though you hate her with the hatred of the adder,
and even in the palm of God. But, in the nights, with that
vision of judgment before me, I know that I hold myself
back. For I hate Florence. I hate Florence with such a
hatred that I would not spare her an eternity of loneli-
ness. She need not have done what she did.

Dowell has moved from paradise to limbo, though
elsewhere again and again, when he has warmed to
his subject, he places himself and the others in hell.
For the moment, he is being tentative, intermediate,
groping for the term *limbo*, incapable of feeling or
knowing. Yet in the next sentence, in an apparent *non
sequitur*, he is not incapable of judging: he merely
assigns the business to God. But he himself can punish

Edward and Florence a little by recalling that they are dead and by being generous to them in their afterlife ("their Judge . . . I hope, will open to them the springs of His compassion"). His punishment of them is incommensurate with what he has been made to endure, and he will do better in a moment; and after he piously conceals, not the nothingness which he feels, but the bitterness, he abandons the conventional moral classification (honest-dishonest, just-unjust) that he sometimes takes up, and goes on to his real business, his vision of the judgment of Florence.

It *is* "almost too terrible," the pride behind the image of judgment that not God but he, Dowell, has created, of Florence alone, excluded as he has been excluded, watching two figures in their embrace, as he has watched and made the reader watch throughout the book, with the eyes of a voyeur. So he pays Florence back in kind. She is made to relive for all eternity the scene that precedes her suicide, when she witnesses Edward's declaration of love to Nancy. Dowell punishes Florence to make her suffer—and to be able to nurse her again. Even in his fantasy, he too must relive the part he plays in life: the repetitions are Dantesque.

To hate or to nurse—to make himself and his passion felt, or to efface himself in a role that both conceals and suggests impotence—he wishes for both and puts aside the conflict with a wry joke: "Well, perhaps they will find me an elevator to run." The presence of these two impulses often accounts for the unevenness in his tone. His moods volatilize rapidly: "No, I do not think that there is much excuse for Florence. . . . He [Jimmy] certainly didn't care for her. Poor thing."

These are opposing impulses, and the conflict is suspended through the action of narration, which puts him in contact with life and enables him to

achieve and master the real world through the pat-
terning of his narrative, to escape from his inner
sepulchre, and to repudiate his former self—the
trained poodle, the child, the old maid, the nun, the
convent, the walking dead, the male nurse in his
shock-proof universe. "What I had to do . . . was just
to get back into contact with life. I had been kept for
twelve years in a rarified atmosphere; what I then had
to do was a little fighting with real life . . . something
harsh, something masculine."

Nowhere is he so effective and so potent as when
he tells the story of Florence's suicide. He tells it su-
perbly, in several places, in language marked by vigor-
ous and incisive imagery, as if in telling it he were
releasing his unused powers to carry out "the business
of the novelist," which is "to make you see things
clearly."

The sovereign's soft, exquisitely trained voice would say:
"Ja, ja, ja!" each word dropping out like so many soft
pellets of suet; the subdued rasp of the official would come
. . . like five revolver-shots; the voice of Monsieur Schontz
would go on and on under its breath like that of an un-
clean priest reciting from his breviary in the corner of a
railway carriage.

Florence, you may also remember, was all in black,
being the mourning that she wore for a deceased cousin.
. . . It was a very black night and the girl was dressed in
cream-coloured muslin, and must have glimmered under
the tall trees of the dark park like a phosphorescent fish in
a cupboard. You couldn't have had a better beacon.

There are other moments when Dowell allows
himself to show us what he is capable of, and they
are always motivated dramatically: there is some reason for the display. On their excursion to M——, for
example, he looks out the train window:

. . . of course, the country isn't really green. The sun shines, the earth is blood red, and purple and red, and green and red. And the oxen in the ploughlands are bright varnished brown and black and blackish purple; and the peasants are dressed in the black and white of magpies; and there are great flocks of magpies too.

Even after he bursts out laughing at a cow that has landed on its back in the middle of a stream, he cannot command the attention of his companions: "no one noticed me." He has a painter's eye for color; he can perceive freshly what they see conventionally. He can see and respond to the landscape, or to a comic situation, when they see nothing; he knows more German and more history than they; but Florence and Leonora vie for the job of cicerone, unaware that he is the man to do it—and Dowell turns to the reader for acknowledgment of his considerable powers, for some redress from the sense of impotence that informs all his relationships within the story.

It is appropriate that Dowell thinks of Edward anachronistically, as the knight and the good soldier; these images belong to a glorious and irrecoverable past, and in their clarity and simplicity, they seem far from the complications of sexual life in the modern world. Dowell and Edward, in their separate ways, seek absolute purity. Dowell can identify himself with Edward by seeing him always as the perfect knight— Lohengrin, Le Cid, Le Chevalier Bayard, the troubadour Peire Vidal, in short the good soldier. In these figures, there is no conflict between sexual success and the spiritual life. Each reinforces the other, and thus Dowell's conflict between sexuality and purity is resolved vicariously for him. At times Dowell is content to be an admirer of Edward's attainments; at other times he would rather *be* Edward.

I suppose that I should really like to be a polygamist; with Nancy, and with Leonora, and with Maisie Maidan, and possibly even with Florence. I am no doubt like every other man; only, probably because of my American origin, I am fainter. At the same time I am able to assure you that I am a strictly respectable person.

—Out of the running, Dowell means to apply what he has to say about love only to Edward, not himself. And just as he knows a good deal about his "unconscious" hatred for Edward ("Perhaps one day when I am unconscious or walking in my sleep I may go and spit upon poor Edward's grave"), he knows a good deal about his "unconscious" identification with him ("I have only followed, faintly, and in my unconscious desires, Edward Ashburnham"). Toward the end it is clear to Dowell that his love for Edward is self-love.

For I can't conceal from myself the fact that I loved Edward Ashburnham—and that I love him because he was just myself. If I had had the courage and the virility and possibly also the physique of Edward Ashburnham I should, I fancy, have done much what he did.

Edward is so much more perfect than he (more manly) that Dowell can love himself only in his idealized form—which he finds in Edward. Dowell's love is always unrequited. On the other hand, Dowell represents the pole toward which Edward moves at the end—toward the atrophy of sexual power through disuse and paralysis. Edward has compartmented his sexual life: Leonora is an object of respect ("she had not for him a touch of magnetism"), and his mistresses are the objects of his sexuality. He is paralyzed by his feelings for Nancy, which cut across the lines he has worked out.

There are moments in the story when Dowell is perfectly honest with himself and with the reader about his need for love. We remember his saying once, "I do not believe that anyone has ever been fond of me." To this Leonora replies—and he reports it— "I'm fond enough of you . . . to say that I wish every man was like you." Again, in his digression on love, he is without irony and without tricks. He simply speaks the truth, and the passage takes on added poignancy because we know how fearful he is of experience, how he instinctively turns away from life.

As I see it, at least, with regard to man, a love affair, a love for any definite woman, is something in the nature of a widening of the experience. . . . A turn of the eyebrow, a tone of the voice, a queer characteristic gesture . . . these things are like so many objects on the horizon of the landscape that tempt a man to walk beyond the horizon, to explore.

In this passage he adumbrates the final passion of Edward and yet makes his definition inclusive enough to contain his own suffering:

But the real fierceness of desire, the real heat of a passion long continued and withering up the soul of a man, is the craving for identity with the woman that he loves . . . there is no man who loves a woman that does not desire to come to her for the renewal of his courage, for the cutting asunder of his difficulties. . . . We are all so afraid, we are all so alone, we all so need from the outside the assurance of our own worthiness to exist.

Love is at once a relief from suffering, a way of taking hold of the outer world and drawing it into the center of one's life—and, as passion, a source of suffering. Edward's passions were "merely preliminary canters compared to his final race with death." "He wore himself to rags and tatters and death—in the effort to leave her [Nancy] alone."

Edward literally dies of love ("I am so desperately in love with Nancy that I am dying of it"), and the

book's romantic quality—that is, its quality of belief
in the importance of the emotional life—comes from
the promise Ford holds out to us that a man can die
of love, as Edward indeed does. And there are moments in *The Good Soldier* when its language recalls
those most romantic of all novels, *Wuthering Heights*
and *Jane Eyre*.

"Nancy, I forbid you to talk about these things. I am the
master of this house." And, at the sound of his voice, heavy,
male, coming from a deep chest, in the night, with the
blackness behind him, Nancy felt as if her spirit bowed
before him, with folded hands. She felt that she would go
to India, and that she desired never again to talk of these
things.

Certainly in its insistence on maleness and female-
ness as the controlling forces of the universe, the
novel links itself to the work of the Brontës. But the
point Ford makes is that Edward as master of the
house is supplanted by Dowell, the antihero, the
American millionaire, whose mastery is both sexless
and meaningless. Again: "He [Edward] appeared as a
man who was burning with inward flame; drying up
in the soul with thirst; withering up in the vitals."
Edward is a romantic hero, romantically conceived,
in an antiromantic universe. Passion must destroy itself. It cannot be salvaged, even through domestica-
tion, as it is in *Jane Eyre*. There can be no happy
ending.

The final situation of *The Good Soldier* is Gothic
in its intensity and atmosphere, its vividness and
delineation of sexual cruelty and masochism. Leonora
digs her sharp nails into her palms. Her cruelty,
aroused by the knowledge that Nancy would make
Edward happy, lies close to the surface. She would like
to bring her riding-whip down on Nancy's face, and
her words leave "a lasting wheal" on Nancy's mind.
Nancy sees her as if she were "a hungry dog . . . a

cruel and predatory beast" that had driven Edward to madness.

In turn, Nancy knows—as well as her alcoholic and estranged and half-mad mother, or Leonora, or anybody else—how to cause as much pain as possible. Being both innocent and cruel, she is doubly effective, and she, in turn, drives Edward to suicide. She is by no means a "symbol of innocence," and the novel is quite explicit about her cruelty. She is only half saint ("that saintly and swanlike being"). She is a "miracle of patience who could be almost miraculously impatient." Half "Maenad," she can also be "unmanned."

The narrator remarks on the contradictions of her convent life and its "mixture of saturnalia and discipline" and of her family life: "she [her mother] sneered at all emotional displays. Nancy must have been a very emotional child." She inherits her violence from a father whom only she can control and who cringes before her—"but she could not have done more to put him at his ease. Perhaps she had had lessons in it at her convent." In such a context, her occasional eruptions of disorder and revolt, for example, her flinging her clothes around her room, are a prefiguring of her madness, that "despairing attempt at revolt."

Defenseless against her because he loves her, Edward seems to "stand, naked to the waist, his forearms shielding his eyes, and flesh hanging from him in rags." Nancy and Leonora "flay" him; they "were like a couple of Sioux who had got hold of an Apache and had him well tied to a stake."

Instinct, cruelty, aggressiveness, sexuality—Dowell would like to know what to make of it all. He has raised the question at the beginning: "There is nothing to guide us. . . . Or are we meant to act on impulse alone? It is all a darkness." And now he asks it again at the end:

It is a queer and fantastic world. Why can't people have what they want? The things were all there to content everybody; yet everybody has the wrong thing. Perhaps you can make head or tail of it; it is beyond me.

Is there then any terrestrial paradise where, amidst the whispering of the olive-leaves, people can be with whom they like and have what they like and take their ease in shadows and in coolness? Or are all men's lives like the lives of us good people—like the lives of the Ashburnhams, of the Dowells, of the Ruffords—broken, tumultuous, agonized, and unromantic lives, periods punctuated by screams, by imbecilities, by deaths, by agonies? Who the devil knows?

Miss Caroline Gordon has observed that, except for Leonora (and Dowell) , the characters get exactly what they want—"death or madness, which is a form of death."[2] Perhaps Ford's point is that men—and women—have contradictory wants, that they both want and do not want what they get, that they wish for their own pleasure and at the same time their own death.

Dowell is able to answer his own question by the end: "Conventions and traditions I suppose work blindly but surely for the preservation of the normal type; for the extinction of proud, resolute, and unusual individuals." He has told his story by means of repetitions, with each repetition not only "casting back" and eddying around to find still another refraction, another context, another link, but strengthening his mastery over his own experience—much as children do through repetition in their play. His answer, when it comes, is toned down by "I dare say" and "I suppose" and his other stock of disclaimers, but his general conclusion fits the facts of the story. It is not all a darkness: civilization *has* given us definite guidelines, though they are in conflict with men's impulses and cause them infinite suffering. Only the toughest—those personalities with the strongest instincts for self-preservation—can survive in a civilized state.

The book is a kind of parable of the struggle of the human species for existence in a civilized state, existence being conceived of as twofold. How to live and live splendidly—one pays with one's life or one's sanity—is a question distinct from how to survive.

The narrator gropes toward definition, and having figured out where Edward and Nancy, Leonora and he himself, "belong" in the scheme of things, he deals with the idea of normalcy as he finds it—to his admiration and horror—in Leonora. Leonora is for him the perfectly normal woman; that is, "in normal circumstances her desires were those of the woman who is needed by society. She desired children, decorum, an establishment; she desired to avoid waste, she desired to keep up appearances." Her cruelty and destructiveness he attributes to "her share of the sex instinct that makes women be intolerably cruel to the beloved person." (Deficient in this instinct, the narrator is therefore less aggressive than other men, and less dangerous.) Leonora emerges from the story not only intact but remarried and pregnant, having pushed Edward to the edge of suicide and Nancy to madness.

Clean-limbed, as we are told over and over, and with a passion for order, Leonora gives Edward such a profusion of initialed pigskin cases for his things that "it must have needed a whole herd of the Gadarene swine to make up his outfit." She makes order both of Edward's financial affairs and of his sexual needs. (Dowell tells us that she pimps for him.) Leonora is the great regulator, the agent of civilization, repairing the damages caused by Edward's instincts, rebuilding the family fortune after his episode with La Dolciquita (that lady who could keep both her appetites and her business affairs in excellent condition). Ironically, Leonora continues to rebuild the family fortune even when there is no longer any need—for the children she never has with Edward. She builds by thrift and investment and renunciation —and as Dowell observes, "In the United States of North America we call it the New England conscience." Her self-denials are extraordinary. She starves her physical passion for Edward, and she cannot respond even to his admiration for her as his business manager:

"By Jove, you're the finest woman in the world. I wish we could be better friends."

She just turned away, without a word, and went to her cabin. Still, she was very much better in health.

She can respond at the end to a second husband, but he is, Dowell assures us, "like a rabbit." During her marriage to Edward, she keeps her mouth shut and her jealousy under control so that all will appear "flawless," perfectly ordered. She cannot stand novels, and she allows herself "no dresses, no jewels—hardly even any friendship, for fear they should cost money." She goes into "retreat"—it was "very good for her health and it was also very inexpensive." But she has fantasies of her husband's sexual excesses. She hates Edward's largesse toward his tenants and his servants, which she rightly equates with his sexual prodigality. She "hated also his deeds of heroism." She cannot understand his sense of gesture, and their first real quarrel is over his wish to honor her by building a Catholic chapel on their estate. His conception of the good landlord and his "violent conviction of the duties of his station" seem to her merely ruinous.

His own theory—the feudal theory of an overlord doing his best by his dependents, the dependents meanwhile doing their best for the overlord—this theory was entirely foreign to Leonora's nature. She came of a family of small Irish landlords—that hostile garrison in a plundered country.

It is a class war as well as a sexual battle that she fights; and in the effort to remake him in her own image and enfeeble him as a man, she takes his work away from him, and with it his honor and his way of life.

> She did not . . . understand that to let Branshaw affected him with a feeling of physical soiling—that it was almost as bad for him as if a woman belonging to him had become a prostitute.

And later

> He hated her when he found that she proposed to set him up as the Lord of Branshaw again—as a sort of dummy lord, in swaddling clothes.

The Victorian gospel of work had been the subject of *Work*, one of Ford Madox Brown's important paintings, with Thomas Carlyle and F. D. Maurice, those great Victorian proponents of work, walking in the foreground. It is significant that Dowell has no work—until he writes his novel. He has done nothing to acquire or to keep his wealth, and he evades even the decision of how to use it. Leonora would remove Edward from his most vital connection with the human community and get him to deny the paternalistic and erotic elements that make up his sense of *noblesse oblige*: he cannot resist giving, and he cannot resist giving comfort with his body.

The deprivations to Edward are never made good, and the extinction of splendid personality, like the fall of a great civilization, is the burden of the book. Leonora, on the other hand, annexing her husband's role as well as his property, gets enough satisfaction for some of her instincts—the urge to acquire, to order, to destroy—to make up for the checking of others. Civilization, she knows, is built up on the renunciation of present happiness for the sake of future security. She

has been raised as a Roman Catholic, and she gets
from religion her habit of belief in future benefits, in
the heaven to come. Her pimping for Edward is "the
cross that she had to take up during her long Calvary
of a life."

Her faith, she tells Dowell, makes her "become
the doormat" for Edward's feet. She keeps her knowledge of the Florence-Edward affair from him because
otherwise those two would "make a bolt of it and . . .
she would lose forever all chance of getting him back
in the end"—for herself and the Church. If she can
see Edward through the long succession of mistresses,
she will get him back, and her triumph will be the
triumph of the Catholic wife.

Religion has not taught her to value this life
less than the next: it has taught her how to be patient
and how to wait for her rewards in this life. So she
does better than any of the others. At the end of the
story she endures, an example of "the preservation of
the normal type." Her sexual experience has been
"impossible to imagine." Until she was married, "you
might almost say that she had never spoken to a man
except a priest." At the time of her marriage and "for
perhaps a couple of years after," neither she nor Edward "really" knew "how children are produced." Yet
she seems to know more about riding the waves than
anyone else. It is the combination of faith and pragma-
tism, innocence and astuteness, that makes her such an
interesting variation of the conventional *femme fatale*,
destroyer of men.

Florence, by contrast, is shamelessly self-indul-
gent. By means of her "heart," the illness she pretends
in order to deceive her husband, she throws off all
traditional restraints: her personality is fundamentally
antagonistic to the very idea of culture—and all the
while, in her predatory way, she bones up on history,

art, architecture, and archaeology, to play the guide through the years at Nauheim. Her elopement is a parody—of the conventional revolt against convention: "We had got married about four in the morning and had sat about in the woods above the town till then, listening to a mocking-bird imitate an old tom-cat." It is a brilliant comic metaphor for Dowell's relation to all experience, not just his honeymoon. The courtship itself—comic, disagreeable ("I was like a chicken that is determined to get across the road in front of an automobile") —precedes what is substantially a *mariage de convenance*, with its "rules" a grotesque parody of the marriage vows.

Florence's suicide has a hard, brittle quality—the sudden crumpling of a surface—and we care as little as we would in "a French comedy. Because of course she was always play-acting." It is the suicide of a materialist and a cold sensualist (Dowell's terms for her), and we respond to her heartlessness with our own. For Dowell, she "just went completely out of existence, like yesterday's paper."

All the other personalities in the story are forced to make some sort of sacrifice to their own desires: they see the justice of certain universal restrictions on their appetites and subscribe to some system of laws. Edward's is an elaborate code, an amalgam of the British schoolboy, the feudal landowner, the medieval knight, the gentleman, the English officer, the hero of sentimental fiction; Leonora and Nancy are practicing Catholics; Dowell, for want of any other connection, is a Philadelphia Quaker. But Florence, we are told, is a Vassar graduate: "You are to imagine that, however much her bright personality came from Stamford, Connecticut, she was yet a graduate of Vassar."

It is a curious mechanism that Dowell shows us:

a woman without any inner controls, who abides by
no system of beliefs except a hocuspocus kind of
"theological" framework based on the significant re-
currence of August 4 in her life: she is born, begins
her affair with Jimmy, marries Dowell, succeeds Mrs.
Maidan as Edward's mistress, and takes prussic acid
—all on August 4. (For Ford, chronicler of civilization, the date had a special point: on August 4, 1914,
England entered World War I.) The system of dates
applies to no one else in the story. It is, Dowell tells
us, "one of those sinister, as if half-jocular and altogether merciless proceedings on the part of a cruel
Providence that we call a coincidence": the pattern-
ing of her life is a parody of the inexorable laws of
retribution. "Florence was a contaminating influence," "Florence was vulgar": in these judgments, as
in his dream, Dowell invents a God so that he can
punish her.

If Dowell makes an avenging God his authority,
Florence makes an impotent husband her authority.
Any outside power over herself that she can accept
must be of her own choosing, and she makes Dowell
the embodiment of the conscience she does not have
but knows she ought to. As long as she can keep him
deceived about her past and her "heart," she can do
what she likes. The construction is at once an exter-
nalization of conscience and a parody.

Ford is so much in possession of his book that the
large element of parody merely illuminates and am-
plifies the central questions raised—without any im-
pairment to the elegiac note. The comedy and the
pain together strike a double note. It is the ambiguous
and beautiful sound that we recognize as distinctively
Fordian and that came from his need to examine both
sides of the subject as fairly as possible. If it left a
good deal unresolved, as some of his critics have
pointed out—where, for example, to place one's sym-

pathy once and for all, or how exactly to interpret matters of tone—it also left the reader with the sense of having had the experience under scrutiny turned to every kind of light.

5

Parade's End

If Ford had put all that he knew into *The Good Soldier*, he put all that he had left into *Parade's End*: it was to be proof not so much of what he could do but of whether or not he could again be a writer at all. Ironically, with his "rich passion . . . for extremes,"[1] he set himself the largest task he had ever taken on. Having come through The Great War battered, gassed, and shell-shocked, he would make one vast effort: it was his "immense big novel," his "ponderous novel," "millions of words" long, as he referred to it in his letters—written on a scale so large that he seemed to have turned the telescope the other way after *The Good Soldier* and looked out over a whole decade, seeing a whole society panoramically—rather than five characters enclosed in the narrator's mind. Ford's "subject" was to be, as he put it later in *It Was the Nightingale*, "the public events of a decade," the world as it culminated in the war." The book was to be a trilogy (originally) that would serve as a history of his own time, and the amplitude of its scale was appropriate to the amplitude of its subject. It was to be his epic.

Parade's End is, of course, a "war novel"—really an antiwar novel, Ford called it, for he intended to show "what war was like" without overstating its physical horrors. W. H. Auden called *Parade's End* a "four-volume study of Retribution and Expiation";[2] Graham Greene read it as a book about the power of a lie.[3] These themes are present, but they are lesser themes. As Robie Macaulay has pointed out, Ford's book is really "more about our own world than his";[4] Ford wrote prophetically about the world he saw and understood. *Parade's End* is about historical change; its theme, most inclusively stated, is the great and irreversible change in human consciousness that took place when the shift from the civilization of the nineteenth century to that of the modern world as we know it occurred under the stress of World War I.

The complicated story of *Parade's End* tells itself in a series of images. At the center is the triangle composed of Christopher Tietjens, the main character; his estranged wife, Sylvia, who pursues him and would destroy him, if she could, and prevent another woman from having him; and Valentine Wannop, the other woman, whom Christopher loves, finally acknowledges to himself that he loves, and lives with after the war.

The secondary yet overlapping story, which takes the form of a seesaw, is of the rise of Vincent Macmaster, son of a poor shipping clerk, and Christopher's corresponding "fall" in the great world of English government and society. The war, with Christopher at the front, is imaged by Ford in explosions, trenches, huts. And after the war, Christopher and Valentine retreat to the English countryside, in *Last Post*, to live their own lives and raise their child.

Parade's End consists of four novels, published as separate volumes (1924–1928) exactly a decade after the war (1914–1918): *Some Do Not . . .* (1924), *No More Parades* (1925), *A Man Could Stand Up—* (1926) , and *Last Post* (1928) . The books were not published in one volume until 1950 in the United States, nor were they known in England as *Parade's*

End. The American title is merciful: even the best-intentioned readers have difficulty remembering and keeping in order the first three teasing, low-keyed, and unwieldy titles. Oddly, Ford was emphatic on two points: it is clear from his correspondence in 1930 (1) that he intended the novels as a trilogy rather than a tetralogy ("I strong wish to omit *Last Post* from the edition. I do not like the book and have never liked it. . . .") and (2) that if the novels were to have one general title, it should not be *The Tietjens Saga*, though Ford had often referred to them as the Tietjens novels. ("I do not like the title *Tietjens Saga*—because in the first place 'Tietjens' is a difficult name for purchasers to pronounce and booksellers would almost inevitably persuade readers that they mean the Forsyte [sic] Saga with great damage to my sales.")

The title *Parade's End* was originally Ford's own suggestion in 1930 and picks up the note of the second volume, emphasizing its title. The words "no more parades" meant, of course, that given the kind of war being waged and the social changes taking place, there would be no more pomp, no more ceremony, no more public processions, no more posturing. Not that the idea of ceremony is contemptible, but by itself, with nothing behind it, it is the outward show of nothing. Having no meaning, it has no reason for being.

"At the beginning of the war," Tietjens said, "I had to look in on the War Office, and in a room I found a fellow. . . . What do you think he was doing . . . what the hell do you think he was doing? He was devising the ceremonial for the disbanding of a Kitchener battalion. You can't say we were not prepared in one matter at least. . . . Well, the end of the show was to be: the adjutant would stand the battalion at ease: the band would play 'Land of Hope and Glory,' and then the adjutant would say: There

will no more parades. . . . Don't you see how symbolical
it was: the band playing 'Land of Hope and Glory,' and
then the adjutant saying *There will be no more parades*?
. . . For there won't. There won't, there damn well won't.
. . . No more Hope, no more Glory, no more parades for
you and me any more. Nor for the country . . . Nor for
the world, I dare say . . . None . . . Gone . . . Napoo
finny* No . . . more . . . parades!"

Professor Fussell, in *The Great War and Modern
Memory* has spoken of "the collision . . . between
events and the public language used for over a century to celebrate the idea of progress."[5] World War I
was a breaking point in European culture, and Ford
was marking the break not only in public events but
in language. By "no more parades" he meant, in addition to the more obvious sense of the phrase, no more
hollow rhetoric, no more heroic abstractions like hope
and glory and honor—an end of traditional moral
language, those words that, compared to the concrete
names of villages, indeed seemed obscene to Hemingway in *A Farewell to Arms*.

To Ford those words seemed extinct, and in
Parade's End his achievement was to render the experience of the war in a language adequate to it and
more accurate than the language inherited from another era. Of the great modernist writers—Joyce,
Eliot, Pound, Yeats, Lawrence—Ford was the only one
to have been involved directly in the war, and he was
alone in bringing to that experience the great technical innovations of twentieth century literature. Aside
from its other merits, *Parade's End* is, for this reason,
historically the most important English novel to come
out of World War I.

---

* "Napoo finny" was the English Tommy's approximation of "Il n'y en a plus" and "fini": "there is no more"
and "finished."

Ford's reasons for disliking *Last Post* were never clear. He tells us that he had originally intended to deal with the period before the war and the war itself, not with the lives of his characters in the years following it. But it may be that his natural preference for the three-part form more than anything else made him regret the actual necessity for the fourth part as it came upon him. In his introductory letter to *A Man Could Stand Up—*, he referred to that volume as "penultimate": obviously, he could not, much as he wanted to, do without *Last Post* and keep to his original three-part idea. The *aba* song form was as inevitable and right for him in the design of his novels as it was in his life: how else account for the curious name he constructed for himself after the war?

No More Parades and *A Man Could Stand Up—* have a clear three-part structure, and *Some Do Not . . .* , while divided into two parts, illustrates the characteristic Fordian return to the opening theme. *Some Do Not . . .* opens—and the first paragraph has been justly celebrated as one of the great openings in the English novel—with two young men, Christopher Tietjens and Vincent Macmaster, riding in the pre-war railway carriage, the leather straps on the windows "of virgin newness," the upholstery "luxuriant" and "regulated" in "an intricate pattern, the design of a geometrician in Cologne," the smooth-running train smelling "hygienically" of varnish—every detail contributing to an image of design, order, opulence, and perfection of surface, all a metaphor for the civilization about to be changed irrevocably.

The end of the novel returns to this scene: Tietjens's mind counterpoises it with the party celebrating Macmaster's knighthood. The two men are once more together. The war has intervened, Macmaster has profited from it (his knighthood is conferred for statistical calculations Christopher had made) , and

Christopher is about to leave for the fighting in France again.

The title of *Some Do Not . . .* , like all the other titles of the tetralogy, recurs throughout the novel, turning up in different contexts, emerging in variations ("Gentlemen don't," "women didn't, "some girls have") and wandering into the other books, there acquiring unexpected, witty, and poignant resonances. "Some do not" is part of a line from Ford's poem "Mr. Bosphorus and the Muses" (1923) . In the title of the novel Ford quotes himself:

> The gods to each ascribe a differing lot:
> Some rest on snowy bosoms! Some do not!

And Macmaster, who, at the opening of the novel misreads the times (he believes a war is impossible) and misreads Rossetti (yet will build his career on his monograph on Rossetti) , misquotes the lines, changing them to

> The gods to each ascribe a differing lot:
> Some enter at the portal. Some do not!

A careerist of the most determined kind, Macmaster characteristically changes the verb and the image, so that the categories refer to success and failure rather than luck. The snowy bosoms are replaced by portals: Macmaster's sexuality, always circumspect, and his well-managed affair with Edith Ethel Duchemin, the wife of the Reverend Duchemin, form the second story of the book, parallel to Christopher's; and each of the stories comments on the other.

Ford could not see the issue of sexual morality apart from that of the war, nor could Christopher.

Macmaster said loftily:
'You're extraordinarily old-fashioned at times, Chrissie. You ought to know as well as I do that a war is impossible—at any rate with this country in it. Simply because . . .' He

hesitated and then emboldened himself: '*We*—the circum-spect—yes, the circumspect classes, will pilot the nation through the tight places.'

And Christopher answers:

'War, my good fellow' . . . —the train was slowing down preparatorily to running into Ashford—'is inevitable, and with this country plumb centre in the middle of it. Simply because you fellows are such damn hypocrites. There's not a country in the world that trusts us. We're always, as it were, committing adultery—like your fellow [Dante Gabriel Rossetti]!—with the name of Heaven on our lips.' He was jibing again at the subject of Macmaster's monograph.

In the figures of Macmaster and Edith Ethel—as well as Christopher's wife, Sylvia, Ford connects the two issues, the sexual conduct of men and women and the world at war. Edith Ethel, "passionately cultured," with the "elegance and portentousness of a funeral horse," and her lover, Macmaster, make a show of Pre-Raphaelite sensibility and English respectability, camouflaging their eroticism elaborately and affectedly with an aesthetic they exploit for their mutual profit—though the sexual antagonism Edith Ethel harbors but will not acknowledge is as immense as her essential vulgarity.

It is this mixture, and not the fact of fornication, that Christopher sees as filthy. Both at the beginning of the story and ten years later, at the end of *Some Do Not . . .* , he declares, with his characteristic preference for clarity in thought and conduct:

I stand for monogamy and chastity. And for no talking about it. Of course if a man who's a man wants to have a woman he has her. And again no talking about it. . . .

And Christopher in fact suffers for monogamy and chastity; the Macmasters pretend to. It is their way of having what they want and not taking the consequences that seems unprincipled to Christopher. "Principles are like a skeleton map of a country—you know whether you're going east or north." Having no principles, only instincts for self-advancement, they become expert social climbers, appropriately representing a government that, in the same way, has deserted the idea of virtue. The Office of Statistics, to which Christopher will not go back, falsifies official figures; England's political strategy in respect to its allies is exploitative and treacherous; the men at Whitehall betray the men at the front and nullify all sacrifice. No more truth and honor: Ford saw a government run by sycophants and cowards feathering their nests in the middle of the war.

In the famous breakfast scene early in *Some Do Not . . .* the Reverend Duchemin's obscenities explode, appalling and testing the excellent manners of the guests, who almost succeed in appearing to ignore what is so unseemly. The scene is a brilliant image of violence erupting that anticipates the larger violence of the coming war and probes with great subtlety the relationship between sexuality, madness, and culture.

Professor Steven Marcus's conclusion to *The Other Victorians* connects the treatment of sexual life with the social criticism of the modern novel. His comment applies strikingly to *Parade's End*.

In the work of the great late nineteenth-century and early twentieth-century avant-garde artists, and in particular among the novelists, the entire fabric of modern society came in for attack. The focus of their assault was the sexual life of the bourgeois or middle classes, as those classes and the style of life they conducted had come to be the prevailing social powers. The difficulties, agonies, contradictions, double-dealings, hypocrisies, inequities, guilts, and confusions of the sexual life of the middle classes were for these novelists not only bad in themselves; they were symbolic of general circumstances of injustice, unpleasantness, demoralization, and malaise which for these artists characterized the world they inhabited. They endorsed a freer sexual life as a good in itself; and they depicted the sexual anguish of modern persons and the sexual hypocrisies and contradictions of modern society not merely for the sake of exposure and sensationalism (although there was that too), but in order to outrage and awaken the society which had imposed upon itself such hideous conditions of servitude. Society being what it is, they were often punished for their efforts, but the work of awakening had been furthered, the work of bringing back into the central discourse of civilization that sexual life upon which it is built and through which it is perpetuated.[6]

". . . You must have a pattern to interpret things by. You can't really get your mind to work without. The blacksmith said: By Hammer and hand all art doth stand!" Toward the end of the fourth novel, *Last Post*, Christopher's dying brother Mark applies the rules of art to life: coherence is necessary, he means, and it must be wrought; it will not come by itself. His words take us back across the four novels to the opening theme, the "intricate, minute" pattern of the upholstery in the railway car, a pattern that will be dissolved by the events of history.

"I think *The Good Soldier* is my best book technically unless you read the Tietjens books as one novel in which case the whole design appears," Ford had written in a letter. The care with which he—and the other great twentieth-century novelists, notably Conrad, Joyce, and Virginia Woolf—approached questions of pattern and technique, was, as it has been pointed out, a response to the disorder presented by the external world.[7] "The most general common characteristic" of modernist writers was "the inverse relation between the rendered aesthetic order and the represented chaos":

The more disordered the world represented, the more ordered the rendering of the work. . . . The very techniques
used to represent a world of dissolving appearances and
discontinuous selves, of crumbling institutions and discred-
ited authorities . . . are also the techniques that bind part
to part and part to whole with an unprecedented adhesive
force.

Ford's impressionism, the literary theory com-
prising the whole set of artistic assumptions that en-
abled him to write his novels, provided the "rules"
for working into coherence the raw material the world
presents. But rather than deal with the raw facts themselves—that is, the phenomena of the external world
—he tried to get at the very nature of experience, to
study the impact of the external world upon human
consciousness. In other words, he was interested not
in "realism" but in psychological reality.

And in rendering the experience of each of his
characters—Tietjens, Sylvia, their son Mark, Valentine, Christopher's brother Mark, Mark's wife, Marie
Léonie—Ford was as much interested in the individual way each mind experienced as in what it experienced. The characteristic sound of its thoughts,
the psychological rhythms of perception and speech,
the special syntax of each separate consciousness—
through these the reader can grasp each character's
unique psychological experience as well as the facts to
which he responds. The reader is forced to stand, with
each of the characters, "at different angles"* to the
perceived world and to experience twice every act of
perception: once with the character, and once for
himself, reassembling all that he has learned from the
implications of the text. In getting the facts, the reader

---

* The phrase is Christopher's in *Some Do Not . . .* ,
Part II, chapter 4.

simultaneously experiences the whole range of the characters' responses to them.

In *Parade's End*, the point of view is not confined to any one character (as it is in *The Good Soldier*), though, as Ford tells us in *It Was the Nightingale*, there was to be a central observer whose attitudes affect the way in which we read the whole story. But *Parade's End* is not *told* by Tietjens, as *The Good Soldier* is by Dowell: rather, Tietjens's story is told through a far-ranging, "authorial," "omniscient" presence who puts together for us a complicated tissue of the consciousness of each of the many characters. The principal relationships are examined by every character, each aware of the other's awareness. The technique provides a set of reflecting mirrors.

Like the French impressionist painters, writers espousing literary impressionism were forced to make a set of quite revolutionary technical innovations.[8] The most far-reaching and dramatic was the breaking up of chronological time or, as it has come to be known, the time shift. Behind the time shift is the principle of juxtaposition. Chronological time is broken up and rearranged so that we are presented with disparate moments, recalled either voluntarily or involuntarily—because two spots of time, two impressions taken together, like two spots of color, acquire more emotional vibrancy and meaning than they have separately. It is really the old and universal principle of contrast—the two stories in a Shakespearean play coloring one another—applied to the surface of time.

In *Parade's End,* Ford created an elaborate design out of the tension between the actual chronology of the many events that take place before, during, and after World War I, and the activity of the perceiving mind of each of the characters experiencing the

events.* Two kinds of time therefore make themselves felt throughout the story—chronological and
experienced time, and their mingling produces what
has been described as a kind of keyboard of all the
tenses of memory. Ford himself develops the analogy
with music: "The motives mingled fugally," he wrote
in *No More Parades*. What we have is a fluid succession of present moments—or, to use another of Ford's
metaphors, a surgical cutting and stitching.

> She said:
> "If we *could* wash out . . ."
> He said, and for the first moment felt grand, tender,
> protective:
> "Yes, you *can*," he said. "You cut out from this after-
> noon, just before 4.58 it was when I said that to you and
> you consented. . . . I heard the Horse Guards clock. . . .
> To now. . . . Cut it out; and join time up. . . . It *can*
> be done. . . . You know they do it surgically; for some
> illness. . . ."

Throughout his work, Ford had often referred to
a wry Chinese proverb, which shrugged off the possibility of finding the good, the true, and the beautiful
in the real world. In *Thus to Revisit* he wrote:

All my life I have been very much influenced by a Chinese
proverb—to the effect that it would be hypocrisy to seek for
the person of the Sacred Emperor in a low teahouse. . . .
It is a bad proverb, because it is so wise and so enervating.

---

* As a result, the many facts of the story are often
hidden or submerged, a difficulty compounded by the overlapping rendering of the material in the interior monologs
of each character. The chronological facts of *Parade's End*
have been admirably set in order by Professor Arthur
Mizener in his afterword to the Signet edition, which is
reprinted in this volume; see appendix.

It has "ruined my career." . . . That meant that it would be hypocrisy to expect a taste for the Finer Letters in a large public; discernment in critics; honesty in aesthetes or literati; public spirit in lawgivers; accuracy in pundits; gratitude in those one has saved from beggary, and so on.

Ford had written *Mr. Apollo* (1908) to consider what could happen if a Greek god came down to the London of that day; *Parade's End* is about a man who is often thought of by the other characters as an Anglican saint. Christopher Tietjens is as close to the Sacred Emperor as Ford dared make him, and the tetralogy traces the course of his realization that the world is no better than a low teahouse. *Parade's End* is then about Christopher's corrected reading of the world, about his grasp of reality, and about his powers of adaptation.

In *The Good Soldier*, Edward's suicide is a way out, but in *Parade's End* the central character cannot escape his situation. Ford will not allow him to: "He must live his predicament down." He must be a survivor and face the world as it is and as it is becoming; what he finds in no way corresponds to the dream of his imagination. Ford's method, to present every viewpoint as fairly as possible, nevertheless gives us Christopher's as the overarching intelligence of the book; his attitudes and feelings, though they are offset by other attitudes and feelings, guide us morally through the four novels, in spite of his virtual absence from *Last Post*.

The actual prototype for Christopher, as we know from *It Was the Nightingale*, was Arthur Marwood, Ford's good friend who had been long dead when Ford began *Parade's End*. Marwood had "the widest and most serene intelligence of any human being I have yet met." Ford could, he claimed, "set" his mind by him. So haunted was Ford by the power of Marwood's intelligence and personality that he listed him among the "revenants": the ghosts of the past who had for him more reality than the men and women he saw every day. Tietjens was to be a recreation of Marwood, and Ford's intention was "to project how this world would have appeared to him today."

The emphasis of the novel is on Christopher's observation and understanding of the world—and consequently on his suffering, the "human tribulations" that, as Ford noted in *It Was the Nightingale*, "are the only things worth writing about," and that came to him as the original material of the book; the character was to carry "a permanent shackle and ball on his leg . . . something of a moral order and something inscrutable." "He was to go through the public affairs of distracted Europe" with a "private cannonball." The two themes—public and private life—are clearly connected here in Ford's account of the genesis of *Parade's End*. The world war and the private battlefield are inseparable from one another, or, as Ford put it, the war was the "outward sign of inward and spiritual disarray": two related wars and their two resolutions, one central figure to bear the double pressure, and two women.

Remarkably unlucky and hard-pressed, in fact overtested by his misfortunes and the strain and anxiety of going through the war, Christopher bears his trials with such "strength of mind and composure" that Ford counted on his stoicism and his "power of cool observation in tremendous crises" to excite the reader's sympathy—as the heroes of other novelists might excite sympathy by their weakness. Christopher is a strong central character, but not a "hero." Ford deliberately avoided the term in his comments on the book: "I was in no mood for the heroic."

My character would be deprived of any glory. . . . He was to be too essentially critical to initiate any daring sorties.

Indeed his activities were most markedly to be in the realm of criticism.

. . . When it seemed to be his duty he would criticise. That would get him, even at the Front, into many and elaborate messes. . . . So I should get my "intrigue" screwed up tighter and always tighter.

The critical spirit would replace the heroic—would indeed become the only form of heroism untainted by anachronism. Tietjens was to be a "sort of lonely buffalo. . . . An exact observer." The novel would show the chasm between the critical attitude (a phrase Ford liked and used as the title of a book of essays in 1911) and the way the world is really run. In *Parade's End*, knowledge and power move unalterably apart.

Perhaps the greatest critical problem the book offers is the character of Sylvia Tietjens. How are we to understand her and her relationship to Christopher? What, by inference, are we to make of Christopher, who married her? She has often been taken to be the embodiment of evil, an allegorical figure, and one of the great *femmes fatales* in literature. How can we square such an image with Ford's novelistic method, which rests upon the idea that the sympathetic imagination can enlarge the reader's capacity for identification with other people and understanding of them?

Ford's idea of the art of the novel derived largely from Flaubert's principle "ne pas conclure." Ford would often quote that phrase, intended for the practicing novelist, and it meant do not sum up a character; do not draw the reader's conclusions for him; allow him to see and understand for himself. Like Flaubert, Ford seldom gives us a complete physical description of a character. Instead, the character— even the way he looks—emerges from different contexts, always freshly to be perceived, and never totally grasped. In this respect Ford's men and women are like human beings outside the novel, at every meeting needing to be reinterpreted and never finally to be wholly understood. More than any character in Ford's novels—that is to say, more than any of the hundreds of characters he created, Sylvia is the most problematic and difficult to understand.

She had first presented herself to Ford's imagination as a pagan goddess. As he tells us in *It Was the Nightingale*, he once saw a woman in the railway station at Amiens:

She was in a golden sheath-gown and her golden hair was done in bandeaux, extraordinarily brilliant in the dimness. Like a goddess come in from the forest of Amiens!

I exclaimed:

"Sylvia!" So I didn't have to cast about for a name.

Sylvan, of the woods: the original shining figure became, before Ford was done with her, a character of tantalizing complexity. "Who is Silvia? What is she?" Shakespeare's song may have had as much to do with Ford's naming her as did the fresh and arrestingly pagan quality of the actual woman he once saw in Amiens.

Early in *Some Do Not . . .* , Sylvia is compared to the mythological Astarte, Phoenician goddess of love and fertility, and Lamia, in Greek stories the witch who sucked human blood. Though the mythic dimension is certainly implied, and at times implied very strongly, Sylvia *is* neither of these. What is significant is her many-facetedness, and it was present in Ford's original inspiration as a quality of light—coruscating, brilliant, flashing different images at different times, now a goddess, at other times a woman, never reducible to a single fixed aspect.

Virgin and courtesan, devil as well as "a picture

of Our Lady by Fra Angelico," she is presented in
paradoxes, with each quality calling up its opposite.
Perverse, unpredictable, her character is "a matter of
contrariety." "To be seductive and to be chaste" is
the condition she aspires to. To do wickedness and
not be wicked: it is a theological distinction she
makes, and perhaps it is the ultimate paradox of her
nature. Ford repeatedly uses the verb *coil* in connection with Sylvia to suggest a snake, yet the imagery
of writhing is, as often as not, connected with her
suffering. And she speaks of the "almost painful emotion of joyful hatred." "Coldly passionate," she goes
to the front to torment and allure Christopher in the
hope of a *rapprochement*. She loves him for his mind,
she says, but she hates his ideas. "There was no end to
the contradiction in men's characters"—or women's.
That she loves him as she does is, of course, "the impossible complication." The character of Sylvia needs
four books to unfold itself, and Ford is at great pains
to present her point of view with scrupulous fairness.

The Tietjens books have been described by Graham Greene as "almost the only adult novels dealing
with the sexual life that have been written in English."
In the story of Sylvia and Tietjens, the relation between the sexes is seen as a condition of warfare.
Christopher's problem *is* "the whole problem of the
relation of the sexes." Sylvia's "sex viciousness," her
"sex ferocity," her "sex cruelty" are plain. But that
repeated note cannot obscure the fact that the struggle between them is neither simple nor one-sided and
that they are two antagonists of considerable subtlety,
whose antagonism is made all the more subtle by the
similarities between them. Their story is a study in
obstinacies—two strong wills engaged in a war. On
the one side Sylvia acts out of a strongly instinctual
nature; on the other side Christopher distrusts his

instincts and acts from a set of principles which, as he comes to recognize, can no longer serve. In order to use them, he is forced to reexamine them.

Curiously, the novel insists on how similar Christopher and Sylvia are. They are both *hallucinés* (Pound's word for Ford), given to actual hallucination. They are both venerators of the ideal of chastity as a state of physical and moral purity. And their sensitivity to one another's psychological processes is expressed by Christopher's compulsion (his "obsession") to shield Sylvia against gossip and slander, and on her side, by her pity and revulsion at how far she has succeeded in destroying him. There are moments when they meet and fight with the "friendly weariness of old enemies." Even their child—the young Mark—speculates about the basis of their enmity.

Questions of . . . sex-attraction, in spite of all the efforts of scientists, remained fairly mysterious. The best way to look at it . . . the safest way, was that sex attraction occurred as a rule between temperamental and physical opposites because Nature desired to correct extremes. No one in fact could be more different than his father and mother—the one [Sylvia] so graceful, athletic and . . . oh, charming. And the other [Christopher] so . . . oh, let us say perfectly honourable but lawless. Because, of course, you can break certain laws and remain the soul of honour.

It is Sylvia who is generally regarded as lawless, but as she sees Christopher, it is he who is immoral. His principles are so baffling—for example, his systematic refusal to stand up for himself—that they make no sense, and they are so outmoded that she cannot even identify them. He "unsettles" society. As Christopher explains to General Campion:

. . . I've no politics that did not disappear in the eighteenth century. . . . I'm a Tory of such an extinct type that she might take me for anything. The last megatherium. She's absolutely to be excused.

Christopher understands her difficulties.

Their relationship began as a "courtship of spiders," with the female enticing the male. Having married Sylvia "on the hop when he was only a kid," as his brother Mark puts it, Christopher forgives her her "sin." (She believed herself to be pregnant after an affair with a man named Drake.) As Sylvia perceives her marriage to Christopher, she is perpetually the woman taken in adultery. Though she grants that Christopher is more Christian than any man she knows, she finds it unbearable that with her he should play the part of Christ. "But our Lord was never married. He never touched on topics of sex."

Christopher is, in his remarkable selflessness and detachment from the world, correctly regarded as a saint, and his wish for saintliness is one of the repeated themes of the book. But Sylvia's view is to be considered. Christopher cherishes forgiveness (and, as Mark realizes in *Last Post,* Christopher cherishes unforgiveness as well), but Sylvia wants neither his forgiveness nor his saintliness. "How could any woman live beside you . . . and be forever forgiven?" If he had denounced her or cursed her, he "might have done something to bring us together." But his aloofness and self-containment—she complains that he closes himself in "invisible bonds"—make him seem merely cold and feelingless, though he is neither.

Everything in his training as an Englishman and a Yorkshireman (a point Ford makes much of) has worked against the ready and spontaneous show of feeling. To make a display of one's deepest emotions is against the rules. His "calculatedly wooden" expression, his "terrifying expressionlessness," make him as much an enigma to Sylvia as she is to him. Intellectual, abstract, he has a monolithic quality she cannot deal with, except to attack it. She perceives him as a rock, a frozen marble statue. His extraordinary self-control, which puts him beyond her reach as he accepts the consequences of her wildest efforts to humiliate and slander him, is, as she understands it, a form of aggression against her, a way of refusing to acknowledge that she can touch him. It is a tacit statement that she is excluded from his life.

Christopher's brother Mark, who is Sylvia's most implacable enemy, understands this: that she is unable to attract her man is the mainspring of her behavior. It is a case of thwarted love become destructive. A woman unused to frustration or failure with men, she is "sappily in love" with him; that she is "forgiven" but not loved by him is the basic fact of their relationship. Jealous even of Christopher's battalion because he cares about his men so deeply, she says to one of them: "I'm glad the captain . . . did not leave you in the cold camp . . . For punishment, you know."

There is something anarchic about Sylvia; her jealousy and destructive passion resist containment. It is not evil as an absolute that she represents, even at her worst, so much as chaos, irrationality, impulse gone berserk. She is an unhappy, even masochistic woman who must have weak things to torture. She sees Christopher "with a mixture of pity and hatred" as a "tired, silent beast" whom she takes pleasure in lashing, as she once thrashed a white bulldog. On the other hand, "Tietjens' words cut her as if she had been lashed with a dog-whip." Ford is suggesting a mysterious identification here.

All the plumb lines are so entangled, as Ford liked to say about human relations and motives, that human behavior seems incapable of simplicity. Though the marriage is improbable from the start, and Sylvia's adultery makes it even more so, Christopher refuses, out of his sense of honor as a gentleman, to divorce her—a refusal that keeps them connected, and at the same time, alienated. The perversities of her nature make it impossible for her to leave him alone, and the game she plays is to torment him, to provoke him into intimacy. Tietjens understands this side of her and calls it "pulling the strings of the shower-bath." Her game is impulsive rather than systematic. She wants to see where and how and whether Christopher is exposed, and she stops only when he seems to have nothing more to lose, having lost money, property, position, and reputation. Her sense of decency makes an attack on Valentine and her baby unthinkable. Besides, by the time of *Last Post,* it seems to her that "God has changed sides."

Christopher's strength inheres in the fundamental principle of his being, his certainty about his own autonomy, his own outlines. Sylvia's sense of herself is a good deal weaker. She wants to possess him, but possession, as she comes to see, is meaningless without self-possession. And rather than fight back, Christopher merely waits for her ("anguish is better than dishonour" is his battalion's motto) to expend herself, as she finally does.

Christopher's metaphor of the shower bath is, in its understatement, intended to deflate Sylvia's effectiveness. But not even his clearness of mind and temperamental affinity with eighteenth-century rationalism can dissipate the sense of evil that hovers around Sylvia. We first see her in Lobscheid, the "last place in Europe" to be Christianized. There, Father Consett, her "saintly" confessor, hears "the claws of evil things scratching on the shutters" and tries to attribute Sylvia's "evil thoughts" to the "evil place" they are in. But the suggestion remains, no matter how much we understand Sylvia's psychology, that Christopher is under her spell and that she herself may be under a spell. The possibility of magic in Sylvia's capacity for destructiveness inheres in the book, emerging often enough to demand interpretation.

Magic has been defined by the late Hannah Arendt as an "intensification of the world to such a pitch of extraordinariness that reality would necessarily fail to come up to its expectations."[9] Sylvia lives in such an intensified world, but not consistently. Standing away from it long enough to try to understand it, she asks:

How was it possible that the most honourable man she knew should be so overwhelmed by foul and baseless rumours? It made you suspect that honour had, in itself, a quality of the evil eye. . . .

No matter how farfetched her charge or inaccurate her aim, her success in hurting Christopher is uncanny and not to be wholly explained in terms of cause and effect. "I have always been superstitious myself and so remain—impenitently," Ford wrote in 1932. "The most rationalist of human beings does not pass his life without saying: 'I am in luck today!' " In *No Enemy* he had spoken of the "type of feeling" that men engaged in agriculture often have and that makes them "so often passionately disagreeable and apparently unreasonable"—the sense of "wrestling with a personal devil," of an "intelligent, malignant . . . being with a will for evil directed against you in person." "I think that, whilst it lasts," he wrote, "it is the worst feeling in the world."

Ford's belief in a kind of animism—really more significant than his nominal Catholicism for an understanding of his novels—that is, his sense of a universe full of unknown and living forces creating "an atmosphere of loaded dice"—is surely at work in his conception of the Catholic Sylvia. Insofar as she suggests Astarte or Lamia, Sylvia is, in spite of her

Catholicism, a creature from the world of romance.
Throughout his long career, the pendulum of Ford's
imagination swung back and forth between two kinds
of fictional reality—the subjective and the objective:
which is to say that he wrote two kinds of fiction—
those he called romances and those he referred to as
novels, and he was usually careful to designate by a
subtitle which was which. Roughly half of his works
of fiction bear the subtitle *A Romance* (*Romance*,
which he wrote with Conrad, surely needed no subtitle) or some equivalent like *An Extravagant Story*
or *A Just Possible Story* or *A Sheer Comedy*. And the
historical novels are often, though not consistently,
designated as romances. What *Parade's End* represents
is a merging of the two genres—the combination of
psychological reality and fantasy in the same framework, a conjunction that offers an interesting critical
problem.

Tietjens has, as in a fairy tale, incurred the
malignity of a dangerous woman. In putting himself
beyond her influence, he moves from the world of
romance, where cause and effect are incommensurate,
to a small corner of the real world. In Ford's early
fairy tales and romances, metamorphoses occur and
miracles heal and bring back to life. The natural law
of cause and effect is suspended, and we are in the
realm of magic and divine intervention, in "that
sacred and beautiful thing Romance," Ford called it.
In *Parade's End*, Tietjens must face the tangled consequences of every small action—his own or Sylvia's
—and live them down, as Ford put it when he dis-
cussed the genesis of the novel in *It Was the Nightingale*. If Tietjens is to have a new life, he must make
it for himself. Ford is clear about keeping Tietjens
in this imperfect world: the resolution of the book
is coincident with Christopher's growing sense of

reality. And *Parade's End*, unlike *The Good Soldier*, is about learning how to live rather than how to die.

As Ford wrote in another context, the purpose of philosophy was "to teach a man how to bear himself during, and what to expect from, life. All else is stamp-collecting."[10]

Christopher can make a new life ("a man could stand up") because of Valentine.

But, positively, she and Sylvia were the only two human beings he had met for years whom he could respect: the one for sheer efficiency in killing; the other for having the constructive desire and knowing how to set about it. Kill or cure! The two functions of man. If you wanted something killed you'd go to Sylvia Tietjens in the sure faith that she would kill it; emotion: hope: ideal: kill it quick and sure. If you wanted something kept alive you'd go to Valentine: she'd find something to do for it. . . . The two types of mind: remorseless enemy: sure screen: dagger . . . sheath!

He can respect both women for their opposite perfections. Sylvia kills; Valentine cures. And he asks: "Perhaps the future of the world then was to women?"

Valentine is a militant suffragette. When we first see her, she is on a golf course where she has been demonstrating for the vote. She is exercising one of the suffragette movement's characteristic tactics— to invade the traditionally male preserve. Ford himself had helped the suffragettes by writing for Mrs. Emmeline Pankhurst, leader of the Women's Social and Political Union, a pamphlet entitled *This Monstrous Regiment of Women* (1913), published by the Women's Freedom League, and he had a strong sense of the women's movement as the beginning of a new consciousness.

Valentine, whose name suggests love, health, and strength, is a fitting heroine for a novel that is as turned toward the future as *The Good Soldier* was turned toward the past. "She would have to be a militant if my book ever came to anything," Ford wrote later. But Valentine is also the daughter of Professor Wannop, the classical scholar, and from him she has received a sound classical education. Her intellectual roots are in the past, and she longs to read Euripides by the Mediterranean. Christopher admires not only her Latin, which is superior to his, but the fact that her head "is screwed on right." Having worked as a "slavey" to support herself and her mother, Mrs. Wannop, the aging and neglected novelist whose work Christopher so much admires, Valentine has a larger firsthand experience of the English class system than Christopher, and a grasp of reality he admires.

I daresay you're a heroine all right. *Not* because you persevere in actions the consequences of which you fear. But I daresay you can touch pitch and not be defiled.

Although Valentine is as unlike Sylvia as to be her mythical opposite (healer vs. destroyer), Ford has not created a simple antithesis. Instead, he deals with a "civilized ambiguity":[11] in many ways they are similar—and unlike Christopher. For example, neither woman can bear the thought of war: both are pacifists, and though Christopher does not share their views, he understands them.

Not three hours ago my wife used to me almost the exact words you have just used. Almost the exact words. She talked of her inability to sleep at night for thinking of immense spaces full of pain that was worse at night. . . . And she, too, said that she could not respect me. . . .

Both are blonde, both are athletes (unlike the slow and heavy Tietjens). Sylvia is strikingly tall and calls Valentine, who is small, a miniature of herself. Both women are presented along with their mothers, so that we see them as daughters. Both express the same irritation with Christopher in the same language. Valentine feels "something devouring" and "overwhelming" in him that "pushed you and your own problems out of the road." She notes his "calculatedly wooden expression and his omniscience" and his "blasted complacent perfections." Like Sylvia, she feels he has insulted her by not making love to her. When they first meet, Valentine says: "I pity your wife . . . The English country male! . . . The feudal system all complete. . . ."

Tietjens winced. The young woman had come a little too near the knuckle of his wife's frequent denunciations of himself.

Ironically, although Sylvia was conceived as a pagan, it is Valentine whose outlook is more authentically pagan. She is free of the burden of sin and the sense of dualism (body and soul leading separate lives) that Sylvia's Catholic upbringing has given her. In Valentine, body and mind work together. She can be as critical as Sylvia of Christopher's faults. But free of Sylvia's conflicts and morbid engrossment in her own capacity to sin, she has no wish to destroy. Harmony, discipline, "bread-and-butter sense": with these qualities she offers Christopher a "little, tranquil, golden spot" in an unstrung world.

In *The Education of Henry Adams*, Adams had asked: "What could become of such a child of the seventeenth and eighteenth centuries, when he should wake up to find himself required to play the game of the twentieth?" As if in answer, Christopher says:

. . . It is not a good thing to belong to the seventeenth or eighteenth centuries in the twentieth. Or really, because it is not good to have taken one's public-school's ethical system seriously. I am really, sir, the English public schoolboy. That's an eighteenth-century product. . . . Other men get over their schooling. I never have. I remained adolescent. These things are obsessions with me.

Christopher suffers from the defects of his qualities, and the scrupulousness with which he has adopted this code of behavior makes him slow to know his own feelings, which are often in conflict with his principles. Sitting on his mind as if it were a horse, "a coffin-headed, leather-jawed charger," he is at the same time aware of and aloof from the claims and needs of his "under mind," with all its repressed impulses. "He occupied himself with his mind. What was it going to do?" He is a man "in need of a vacation from himself," as he realizes. Under the double stress of the war and Sylvia's harassment, his mind becomes more and more detached until he sees his own dissociation as a danger signal, a portent of the madness he fears.

His decision to live with Valentine is a way of freeing himself and healing himself so that he can adapt to a new set of conditions. "Today's today," he tells himself. "The world was changing and there was no particular reason why he should not change with it." His brother Mark refuses to change; his muteness is a refusal to speak in a world he has come to loathe and despair of, and he wills his own death. In his book on Henry James, Ford had spoken of "the journey towards an entire despair or towards a possible happiness." It is toward the possible happiness that *Parade's End* moves.

. . . He would no longer stand unbearable things. . . . And what he wanted he was prepared to take. . . . What he had been before, God alone knew. A Younger Son? A Perpetual Second-in-Command? Who knew? But to-day the world changed. Feudalism was finished; its last vestiges were gone. It held no place for him. He was going—he was damn well going!—to make a place in it for . . . A man could now stand up on a hill, so he and she could surely get into some hole together!

Christopher has inherited, through the deaths of his older brothers, the vast ("between forty and sixty rooms") Yorkshire estate of Groby that his family had acquired at the time of William of Orange. He renounces Groby because his disaffection with his own class makes it impossible for him honestly to accept its privileges, not the least of them being the immense income the estate yields. But more importantly, by giving it up, Christopher divests himself of the whole unwieldy feudal structure he has inherited. In exchange, he can, for the first time, recognize the legitimacy of personal happiness; "noblesse oblige" comes to include the obligation to oneself.

Christopher has learned that his sanity and his life depend on knowing what to preserve from the past and what to discard. He would like to keep "the old goodnesses"—without their old trappings and parade. And he reinterprets—by the spirit rather than the letter—the laws that have kept him second-in-command of his own life. Salvaging himself from the wreckage, he trims and consolidates his world, selling what is left of his beautiful old furniture, withdrawing from public life to a private life of "infinite conversations," a life of frugality, self-sufficiency, and comparative serenity. He will live his own life, rather than a predetermined model of it—and it will have order and meaning.

"In contentment live obscurely the inner life," Ford wrote later in *Provence*. In *Last Post,* we see Christopher mislaying some precious old prints and Valentine ashamed of the condition of her underthings and Sylvia and her entourage invading the landscape: Ford cannot offer an ideal solution for Christopher and Valentine, and that is the point. He makes it clear in his dedicatory letter to *Last Post:* "And so he will go jogging along with ups and downs and plenty of worries and some satisfactions, the Tory Englishman, running his head perhaps against fewer walls, perhaps against more. . . ." His descendants will carry on the country "without swank."

Christopher has to rethink his connection with the life he has been born to, and for that way of life Ford created one of the memorable symbols in modern literature, that of Groby Great Tree. The tallest cedar in Yorkshire, the fantastic tree was planted to commemorate the birth of Christopher's great-grandfather who "had died in a whoreshop." The tree was said never to forgive the Tietjens family for transplanting it from Sardinia, and it was connected with the family's bad luck, darkening the windows of the house and tearing chunks out of its foundations.

. . . Groby Great Tree overshadowed the house. You could not look out of the school-room windows at all for its great, ragged trunk and all the children's wing was darkened by its branches. Black . . . funeral plumes. The Hapsburgs were said to hate their palaces—that was no doubt why so many of them . . . had come muckers. At any rate they had chucked the royalty business.

Though the tree "did not like the house," Mark knows how much Christopher loved the tree. He would "pull the house down if he thought it incommoded the tree. . . . The thought that the tree was under the guardianship of unsympathetic people would be enough to drive Christopher almost dotty."

The spell is broken through Sylvia's agency, as a final act of revenge on Christopher for the peace he and Valentine share. Sylvia allows the tenant who was renting the ancestral house "furnished" to have the tree cut down—"to suit the sanitary ideas of the day."

It is cut down before Christopher can intervene. The act cannot be undone, and Sylvia, recognizing this, assigns the part to an American. But the curse is removed, as she realizes: "God was lifting the ban." And ironically, Sylvia is the agent by whom the curse of the past is removed.

The ancestors against whom she sins had taken Groby from its rightful owners when the first Tietjens had come over from Holland with William III. The tree, with its great roots and yet its baleful influence, is an ambiguous symbol of the past. In any case, the tree will not darken the house for the generations to come.

Just before Mark dies, Valentine asks him "How are we to live? How are we ever to live?" Her question too is ambiguous, and at last breaking his silence, he answers indirectly, in the old Yorkshire dialect.

> He whispered:
> " 'Twas the mid o' the night and the barnies grat
> And the mither beneath the mauld heard that."
> . . . "An old song. My nurse sang it. . . . Never thou let thy barnie weep for thy sharp tongue to thy goodman. . . . A good man! . . . Groby Great Tree is down. . . ."

Thinking of the future—Valentine's unborn child—Mark reverts to the oldest words he knows. They express the wisdom of the past, the wisdom of the folk. Having heard them as a child from his nurse, Mark uses them to express the continuity of the generations. To Valentine's question "How are we to live?" he answers—in harmony with Christopher, for the sake of the child. The message is for the future, and since he and Marie Léonie have no children, it is clear to Valentine why she should not tell Lady Tietjens of his last words.

> She would have liked to have his last words. . . .
> But she did not need them as much as I.

Epilogue

In his critical monograph *Hans Holbein the Younger* (1905), Ford wrote of Holbein's achievement as an artist:

. . . Holbein's works may be said to have compelled us to look at things as we do, just as, after Palestrina, the ears of men grew gradually accustomed to hear music only in the modern modes. . . . He [Holbein] has redeemed a whole era for us from oblivion, and he has forced us to believe that his vision of it was the only feasible one. This is all that the greatest Art can do. . . .

This statement is perhaps one of the best definitions of style we have, and it applies as well to Ford's own achievement.

His achievement, however, has not been given the recognition it deserves. Criticism and literary history have not yet done justice to Ford, in spite of a group of academic studies in the last twenty years, many of them very valuable. The full impact of Ford's artistic legacy has not yet been felt, and his part in the "march" of literature (he liked to think of art as moving toward an ideal point) is not yet generally known or appreciated.

Why Ford is not, by common consent, acknowledged as one of the great figures of twentieth-century literature raises questions about the nature of the judgments that lie behind the establishment of the literary canon.

For one thing, Ford was as subtle a writer as he was voluminous, and the reading public did not respond kindly to such a combination of demands. His art depends on indirection: digressions, juxtapositions, disjunctions, refractions, obliquities. The critical problems *The Good Soldier* presents can be found all through his work in all the genres he used—novel, memoir, criticism, poetry—and the sheer size of his output has discouraged most readers from giving his books the kind of close reading they demand.

Besides, Ford himself dismissed as negligible most of the novels he wrote before *The Good Soldier*; if he had not written them off, perhaps his readers would have been readier to give them the close attention they require. In any event, Ford did himself incalculable harm. His other disservices to himself would make an impressive list, but his self-denigration was perhaps the most damaging.

Ford was an extremely modest man, in spite of the posing some of his contemporaries reported. As Henry James said of Hawthorne, his modesty was "in excess of his discretion." It embarrassed Ford to write about his own work: his idea of what a gentleman's attitude should be (he should never put himself forward) and perhaps the wish to conceal his true self (rather than expose it publicly) made him adopt what Granville Hicks rightly called an asinine tone about himself.[1]

Like all other artists, Ford led two lives. One was a daily life, in which he wrote letters to his literary agents and publishers, carried on his business, and presented himself to the outside world, sometimes irritatingly in one pose or another, often outrageously in anecdotes at odds not only with documentable facts but with one another. But his other life was more real for him, and it was his life as a writer. He wrote in an early article "Authors' Likenesses and a Caricaturist" (1907) :

I am inclined to shrink from looking at portraits of literary men. For the writer is expressed by his books, and within the four-square of them his whole personality is contained.

More than most writers, Ford has suffered from the failure of his critics to keep this simple matter straight—as one should, he once suggested, "cleanse a saucepan of onions before setting to work to boil milk in it."

Camouflaging the seriousness and intensity of his creative efforts, Ford succeeded in creating an impression of casualness about his work. In his dedicatory letter to Stella in the 1927 edition of *The Good Soldier*, he reported: "I had written rather desultorily a number of books—a great number—but they had all been in the nature of *pastiches*, of pieces of rather precious writing, or of *tours de force*." He did not mean that he had written carelessly: in fact he rewrote *The Benefactor* four or five times. What he did mean was that his earlier novels seemed to him meager by comparison with the possibilities he sensed he could realize—and did. "I had never really tried to put into any novel of mine *all* that I knew about writing." His modesty, however, did him no good with the reviewers, who took him at his own evaluation, relieved to have to look no further.

When he did allow himself a few admiring remarks for what he had achieved in *The Good Soldier*, he referred to them as the "complacencies of an extinct volcano"—this in 1927, with at least eighteen more published books ahead of him, several unpublished manuscripts, and plans toward the end of his life to start another literary review. He seemed to have been pleased with *The Young Lovell*: it "is really literature," he wrote in a letter in 1913, "and I have spread myself enormously over it." He felt that his late novels *The Rash Act* and *Henry for Hugh* were his best books—"at any rate they fill exactly my ideas of what a novel should be." But the impression he created for the world at large, that his books were "trivially suave" and "entirely negligible," seems to have stuck. His disparagement of the historical romance as a genre is better remembered, unfortunately, than his use of it: *The Young Lovell*, his most metaphysical novel, is almost unread today.

The German poet Goethe recognized how easily a literary reputation can be damaged once the process of detraction begins. Goethe was thinking of Diderot, who, as it turns out, was one of Ford's favorite novelists, but Goethe could have been writing about Ford: ". . . And thus, without further scrutiny, the glory of an eminent man is weakened."[2]

Ford spoke often of "self-effacement": it was the first thing a novelist should learn. What he really meant was that the novelist must "render" and "present" his story, not interject himself directly as a presence commenting on it. (He objected to George Eliot and Thackeray on this ground.) But Ford helped to efface his own reputation away. A messy divorce that drew much too much attention from the press and the personal and rancorous attacks on him by Joseph Conrad's wife, Jessie,* further damaged him in the Edwardian literary world. A good deal of the condescension toward him adopted by the English at that time (almost seventy years ago) still survives, and the personal discrediting he suffered, particularly

---

* She lashed out at Ford after his book on Conrad for what she took to be a misrepresentation of his literary relationship with Conrad.

among English critics, continues as a stock response to
Ford—and a substitute for literary criticism.

From the beginning, the assessment of Ford's art
seems to have been hopelessly and oddly entangled
with irrelevancies. Criticism has largely interested itself and weighed itself down, been misdirected and
in fact replaced by the question of whether or not
the stories Ford told about himself and his contemporaries in his memoirs were "true" or accurate. Too
often the issue has been the truthfulness of his anecdotes rather than the truths of his novels. If the
anecdotes Ford told and the facts he supplied in his
autobiographical writing are not to be trusted, why,
it has been implicitly asked, should we take him seriously as a writer—and accord him the attention a
serious writer deserves?

Ford was often accused of lying and had a reputation as a liar, and there is no doubt that he invented.
He has also been called "one of the great anecdotists
of our literature." How are we to regard the problem?

Aristotle spoke of the poet as one who has mas-
tered the art of telling lies successfully. Picasso praised
the lie that makes us see the truth, or makes the truth
better than it is. The poet J. V. Cunningham has
written:

> But memoir in fictitious guise
> Is telling truth by telling lies.

Robert Lowell reported about Ford: "His marvelous,
altering stories about the famous and colorful were
often truer than fact."[3] It would seem then that Ford
has strong support for his creative use of the possibilities of the lie.

Certainly he never felt constrained by fact—by
fact as it is commonly defined. Answering objections
to his inaccuracies, he was "absolutely impenitent."

What he was after, he insisted, was the sense of fact, the impression, as he called it (it should be remembered that he and Conrad thought of themselves as impressionists), that fact makes on the mind rather than fact itself: not the literal truth but *la vraie vérité*. The distinction goes back to Walter Pater and ultimately to De Quincey and his conception of the literature of power and the literature of knowledge. Pater spoke of "soul-fact," and the term has a strangely contemporary sound.

Ford entitled one of his volumes of memoirs *Memories and Impressions* in the American edition and gave it the subtitle *A Study in Atmospheres*. His wish, and his achievement, were to put down on paper not the world but his memories and impressions of it, its atmosphere and quality as it registered itself on his particular sensibility. He offers us the "impression of a man who has spent the great part of his life in recording impressions with an extreme exactitude": that is his claim. William Carlos Williams understood Ford's idea of exactitude. It had to do with the "re-attachment of the word to the object"—"respect for the meaning of words," as Williams explained: "and what a magnificent use they are put to in his [Ford's] hands!"[4]

Ford wrote brilliantly about the art of translation, and his analysis of the problems of translating the opening sentence of Flaubert's story "Un Coeur Simple" ("A Simple Heart") is a model of both commentary and translation.[5] How to render as accurately and clearly as possible not the literal words themselves but the real meaning, the spirit of the passage? He distrusted literalness as other men distrust any departure from it. His contemporaries, reacting to his exaggerations and tall stories no doubt felt, with some justice, when they figured in his stories, that they had lost their real identities, and

Appendix

‿‿‿‿‿‿‿‿‿‿‿‿‿‿‿‿‿‿‿‿‿‿‿‿‿‿‿‿‿‿‿‿

Chronological Sequence
of events in *Parade's End*
by Arthur Mizener

The story begins at the end of June, 1912, when
Christopher Tietjens (twenty-six years old and the
youngest child of an old Yorkshire family of four sons
and two daughters) and Vincent Macmaster are traveling down from London to Rye to play golf and to
interview a man named Duchemin, who has known
Rossetti, about whom Macmaster has been writing a
monograph in the hope of gaining promotion in the
Imperial Department of Statistics, for which both
young men work. Christopher's wife, Sylvia, had run
off four months earlier with a man named Perowne.
Sylvia, who is four years older than Christopher, had
trapped him into marriage when she thought herself
—mistakenly as it turns out—pregnant by an earlier
lover. She has just written Christopher that she wishes
to return to him, having with some difficulty escaped
from the violently possessive Perowne at a town called
Yssingueux-les-Pervenches and joined her mother,
who has been living at a German air resort named
Lobscheid pretending for the benefit of London society that Sylvia is with her. Sylvia has just ordered
Christopher to come to Lobscheid and get her. It is
his worry over this problem, complicated for him by
his idealistic Tory conception of the gentlemanly attitude in sexual relations and marriage, that makes him
so furiously impatient with Macmaster's laboriously

pretentious essay on Rossetti and his later Pre-Raphaelite "gurglings" over Mrs. Duchemin.

On the following Saturday the two young men breakfast at the Duchemins, and that same night Christopher and Valentine take their memorable drive to deliver Gertie Wilson, Valentine's suffragette friend, to Valentine's uncle's house some thirty miles away. On the following Tuesday, at five-fifteen A. M., Christopher leaves to join Sylvia at Lobscheid. His plan is that they shall make an appearance at Wiesbaden to quiet any possible gossip. But when he arrives at Lobscheid, he receives word that his mother has died, apparently of a heart broken by the knowledge that Sylvia is returning to Christopher. Christopher cannot then take Sylvia to Wiesbaden, since they have to go into mourning; he cannot take her to England because he will not have her at his beloved mother's funeral. He therefore takes her on an extended trip to Kiev.

From then until 1915 Christopher and Sylvia, though they do not live together as husband and wife, keep up the appearance of marriage. Just before the outbreak of the war, in July, 1914, they are visiting at Bamborough to go and stay at a nearby cottage where his sister Effie has been caring for their child since Sylvia's escapade with Perowne in 1912. (Somewhat confusingly, this child is called Tommie in *Some Do Not . . .* , later Michael, and later still, Mark, though in *Last Post* it is explained that he was originally christened Mark and renamed Michael by Sylvia when he was received into the Catholic Church.)

While Christopher is with his sister, Macmaster arrives, much agitated because he and Mrs. Duchemin have been spending what they intended to be a quiet lovers' weekend together and have been discovered by friends who may at any minute realize that they are lovers. To help them out of this difficulty, Christopher

escorts Mrs. Duchemin back to London. It is August
3, 1914, the day war was declared, and everyone who
is anybody is on the train hurrying back to London;
they all see Mrs. Duchemin weeping on Christopher's
shoulder and this starts the rumor that Mrs. Duchemin is Christopher's mistress, which Sylvia keeps
alive for the rest of *Parade's End*.

Christopher continues to work in the Imperial
Department of Statistics for a little more than a year
after the war starts, but by the fall of 1915 he cannot
any longer bear faking statistics to help the British
government blackmail France. In November, 1915, at
one of Macmaster's receptions, where Mrs. Duchemin
presides with all her Machiavellian skill in assisting
Macmaster to climb to the top, Christopher tells
Valentine he cannot reconcile it with his conscience
not to enlist. He reaches the front early in 1916 and
is in the fighting throughout that year. Early in 1917,
he is shell-shocked and invalided home. In August,
1917, he is declared fit again and is returned to France,
though his memory is still gone. When he goes, Sylvia
retires to a nunnery at Birkenhead, where she stays
for two and a half months reading prewar romances.

Shortly after Christopher's arrival in France he is
hospitalized with lung trouble, but a month after his
return he is back on duty, in command of a staging
base for new drafts, near Rouen, where Brigadier-
General Campion has his headquarters. With the help
of Perowne, who is on Campion's staff, Sylvia makes
her way to Rouen in November in pursuit of Christopher. There she gets Christopher into such trouble
that General Campion relieves him of his base command and sends him to the front as second in command of the Ninth Glamorganshires. He goes up February 14, 1918, and fights through the great battle of
that spring. In April, during the crisis of the battle,
he is forced by the collapse of the commanding colonel

to take over the battalion. Three days later General Campion relieves General Perry ("Old Puffles") of command of the whole army and immediately takes Christopher's battalion away from him and sends him to command a prisoner-of-war detail.

Early in the autumn Christopher is back in the hospital with lung trouble, and from there, in October, he is sent to a depot at Ealing. On October 20 he goes to see his brother Mark, who is in bed with pneumonia and may die, and persuades Mark to marry his longtime mistress, Marie Léonie Riotor. For the next three weeks Christopher helps nurse Mark; and Mark, to Christopher's financial distress, uses his influence to get Christopher demobilized just before Armistice Day.

On Armistice Day Christopher, needing money, starts out from the house in Gray's Inn with the only piece of furniture Sylvia has left in it, an eighteenth-century cabinet, to try to sell it to Sir John Robertson, who had once offered one hundred pounds for it. He meets Valentine as he comes out the door and tells her to go upstairs and wait for him. Sir John—since taught by Sylvia to hate Christopher—now offers five pounds for the cabinet. Christopher then carries it to Mark's house, where he arrives shortly before noon. Mark refuses to lend him money on the cabinet, insisting that he accept his share of the Groby estate, which he will not do. *Pour le dieu d'amour,* Marie Léonie lends him forty pounds.

Christopher then returns to Gray's Inn, and he and Valentine, together with Aranjuez, his Nancy, and "the pals," go out to dinner to celebrate the armistice; as they are driving home afterwards, Christopher's ex-colonel dies in the cab. Valentine and Christopher finally arrive back at Gray's Inn and are met there by Sylvia, who announces that she is dying of cancer, pretends to faint, and falls down the stairs, putting her ankle out of joint. Valentine fiercely insists that Christopher not assist Sylvia but return with her to Mark's house, where they arrive at two in the morning. When they finally leave for Christopher's house once more, Marie Léonie receives a call from Lord Wolstonmark in Mark's office announcing that the allies are not going to occupy Berlin. When she conveys this information to Mark he has a stroke. Marie Léonie calls Christopher and Valentine and they return. Thus passes their "honeymoon."

Last Post picks the story up six months later [sic], about June, 1920. During the interim Sylvia has first played sick and then started divorce proceedings, not intending to carry them through (she is a Catholic) but wanting her lawyer to have a chance to malign Christopher publicly. During the single afternoon covered by the present time of *Last Post* Sylvia is overwhelmed by the discovery that Valentine is pregnant and by a vision of Father Consett, her confessor, who had been killed with Roger Casement; she decides to give up her war against Christopher and to leave him and Valentine in peace. Mark, no longer having to "will against" her, dies.

Parade's End concludes with Christopher and Valentine struggling to build up the new life for Chrissie to inherit. At the same time, the sustaining will of the old life dies in Mark, and it has no heir, literal or figurative, because Sylvia's son by Christopher refuses Sylvia's name for him (Michael) and dissociates himself from Sylvia's attack on Valentine and Christopher. Even those who cling to the Edwardian way of life have lost faith in it: General Campion, still helplessly charmed by Sylvia, has ceased to believe Sylvia's more and more desperate lies about Christopher; and Sylvia herself, losing all hope of winning her war against Christopher, decides to marry Campion and go with him to India, that last, dying satrapy of Edwardian empire, where what even Sylvia knows now to be the meaningless parade of the old life can be continued for a little while.

Notes

1. TOWARD AN APPRECIATION OF FORD

1. Ezra Pound, *The Letters of Ezra Pound* 1907–1941, ed. D. D. Paige (New York: Harcourt, Brace, 1950), pp. 388–389. "Status Rerum," *Poetry, A Magazine of Verse,* I, 125–126 (January, 1913). *Polite Essays* (Norfolk, Conn.: New Directions, 1937), p. 58. Ibid., p. 50. Ibid., p. 9. *Letters,* p. 419.
2. Hugh Kenner, *Gnomon* (New York: McDowell Obolensky, Inc., 1958), p. 145.
3. Hugh Kenner, *The Poetry of Ezra Pound* (Norfolk, Conn.: New Directions, 1953), p. 264.
4. Richard Aldington, *Life for Life's Sake* (New York: Viking, 1941), p. 158.
5. Lloyd Morris, *A Threshold in the Sun* (New York and London: Harper's, 1943), pp. 217–218.
6. Robert Lowell, Introduction to *Buckshee* (Cambridge: Pym-Randall Press, 1966), xii.
7. Gabriel Josipovici, *The World and the Book* (London: Macmillan, 1971), pp. 259–260.
8. Ford Madox Ford, "The Serious Books," *Piccadilly Review* (November 6, 1919).

2. HIS LIFE

1. Quoted material that follows in this section on Ford's childhood is largely drawn from *Ancient Lights, Re-*

turn to Yesterday, It Was the Nightingale, and *Provence.*

2. Juliet Soskice, *Chapters from Childhood: Reminiscences of an Artist's Granddaughter* (London: Selwyn and Blount, 1921), p. 1.

3. Francis Hueffer, *Italian and Other Studies* (London: Elliot Stock, 1883), pp. 106–107.

4. Soskice, *Chapters from Childhood,* p. 30.

5. Ibid., pp. 235–236.

6. Ibid., p. 32.

7. Edward Dahlberg, *Alms for Oblivion* (Minneapolis: University of Minnesota Press, 1964), p. 14.

8. Letter to Edward Garnett, May 5, 1928, quoted in Arthur Mizener, *The Saddest Story* (New York and Cleveland: The World Publishing Company), p. 55. Quotations from Ford in this section on Conrad are drawn from *Joseph Conrad: A Personal Remembrance, Return to Yesterday, Portraits from Life,* and Ford's Introduction to Conrad's unfinished story *The Sisters* (New York: Crosby Gaige, 1928).

9. *Between St. Dennis and St. George,* p. vi.

10. Todd Bender, "Literary Impressionism: General Introduction," p. 1. Preliminary Papers for Seminar #8, Modern Language Association Annual Meeting, 1975.

11. H. G. Wells, *Experiment in Autobiography* (New York: The Macmillan Company, 1934), p. 527.

12. Samuel Hynes, *Edwardian Occasions* (New York: Oxford University Press, 1972), p. 65.

13. D. H. Lawrence, *The Collected Letters of D. H. Lawrence,* ed. Harry T. Moore (New York: Viking, 1962), pp. 98–99.

14. Hugh Kenner, *The Pound Era* (Berkeley and Los Angeles: University of California Press, 1911), p. 278.

15. Ibid., p. 553.

16. Mizener, *The Saddest Story,* p. 583.

17. Cited in David Dow Harvey, *Ford Madox Ford, 1873–1939: A Bibliography of Works and Criticism* (New York: Gordian Press, 1972), p. 372.

18. William Carlos Williams, *Selected Essays* (New York: Random House, 1954), p. 319.

19. Ford's thumbnail retrospective sketch appears in *Por-traits and Self-Portraits*, collected and illustrated by Georges Schreiber (Boston: Houghton Mifflin Company, 1936), pp. 39–40.

20. Graham Greene, *The Lost Childhood and Other Essays* (New York: The Viking Press, 1952), p. 89.

3.   SOME ASPECTS OF THE OEUVRE

1. Grover Smith, *Ford Madox Ford* in *Six Modern British Novelists*, ed. George Stade (New York and London: Columbia University Press, 1974), p. 104.

2. Frank Macshane, *The Life and Work of Ford Madox Ford* (New York: Horizon Press, 1965), pp. 135 and 172.

3. See *Women and Men* and *Return to Yesterday* (Part Three, chapter one "Cabbages and Queens").

4. Reprinted in Frank Macshane, *Ford Madox Ford: The Critical Heritage* (London and Boston: Routledge and Kegan Paul, 1972), pp. 51–54.

4.   THE GOOD SOLDIER

1. Bender, op. cit., p. 1.

2. Caroline Gordon, *A Good Soldier* (Davis: University of California Library, 1963), p. 22.

5.   PARADE'S END

1. The phrase is Henry James's, from *The Art of the Novel* (New York: Charles Scribner's Sons, 1953), p. 31. Although James is not speaking of Ford, the phrase applies.

2. W. H. Auden, "Il Faut Payer," *Mid-Century*, #22, p. 3 (February, 1961).

3. Graham Greene, Introduction to *The Bodley Head Ford Madox Ford* (London: The Bodley Head, 1962), p. 10.

4. Robie Macaulay, Introduction to *Parade's End* (New York: Alfred A. Knopf, 1950), p. vi.

5. Paul Fussell, *The Great War and Modern Memory* (New York and London: Oxford University Press, 1975), p. 169.

6. Steven Marcus, *The Other Victorians* (New York: Basic Books, 1966), pp. 284–285.

7. This idea is developed by Professor George Stade in his Introduction to *Six Modern British Novelists*, op. cit., p. x. The two quoted statements that follow are his.

8. I am indebted to Professor Bender for his discussion of this matter in his essay on literary impressionism, op. cit.

9. Hannah Arendt, *Rahel Varnhagen* (New York: Harcourt Brace Jovanovich, 1974), p. 60.

10. *When Blood Is Their Argument*, p. 267.

11. The phrase is Professor Fussell's, op. cit., p. 80.

6. EPILOGUE

1. Granville Hicks in "Homage to Ford Madox Ford—a Symposium" in *New Directions: Number Seven* (Norfolk, Conn.: New Directions, 1942), p. 449.

2. Cited in Denis Diderot, *Oeuvres Complètes de Diderot,* ed. J. Assézat (Paris: Garnier Frères, 1875), p. 375.

3. Robert Lowell, Introduction to *Buckshee,* op. cit., xii.

4. William Carlos Williams, *Selected Essays,* op. cit., pp. 321–322.

5. "Un Coeur Simple," *Outlook* (London), XXXV, 738–739 (June 5, 1915).

Bibliography

1. FORD'S BOOKS

The standard bibliography—and an indispensable book for readers of Ford—is David Dow Harvey's *Ford Madox Ford: 1873–1939: A Bibliography of Works and Criticism*. Princeton: Princeton University Press, 1962. The following chronological list of Ford's books follows Harvey's bibliography.

The Brown Owl. London: T. Fisher Unwin, 1891. Children's fairy-tale.

The Feather. London: T. Fisher Unwin, 1892. Children's fairy-tale.

The Shifting of the Fire. London: T. Fisher Unwin, 1892. Novel.

The Questions at the Well [pseud. "Fenil Haig"]. London: Digby, 1893. Poems.

The Queen Who Flew. London: Bliss, Sands, and Foster, 1894. Children's fairy-tale.

Ford Madox Brown. London: Longmans, Green, 1896. Biography.

Poems for Pictures. London: John MacQueen, 1900. Poems.

The Cinque Ports. London: Blackwood, 1900. "A Historical and Descriptive Record" (sub-title) of Kent and Sussex port towns.

The Inheritors. London: Heinemann, 1901. Novel, written in collaboration with Joseph Conrad.

Rossetti. London: Duckworth, 1902. Art criticism and biography.

Romance. London: Smith and Elder, 1903. Novel (historical adventure story), written in collaboration with Joseph Conrad.

The Face of the Night. London: John MacQueen, 1904. Poems.

The Soul of London. London: Alston Rivers, 1905. Sociological impressionism.

The Benefactor. London: Brown, Langham, 1905. Novel.

Hans Holbein. London: Duckworth, 1905. Art criticism.

The Fifth Queen. London: Alston Rivers, 1906. Novel (historical romance; first of the "Katherine Howard" trilogy).

The Heart of the Country. London: Alston Rivers, 1906. Sociological impressionism.

Christina's Fairy Book. London: Alston Rivers, 1906. Children's fairy-tales.

Privy Seal. London: Alston Rivers, 1907. Novel (historical romance; second of the "Katherine Howard" trilogy).

England and the English. New York: McClure, Phillips, 1907. Sociological impressionism; published only in America; composed of the previously published *The Soul of London* and *The Heart of the Country* plus *The Spirit of the People*.

From Inland. London: Alston Rivers, 1907. Poems.

An English Girl. London: Methuen, 1907. Novel.

The Pre-Raphaelite Brotherhood. London: Duckworth, 1907. Art criticism.

The Spirit of the People. London: Alston Rivers, 1907. Sociological impressionism; previously published, only in America, in *England and the English*.

The Fifth Queen Crowned. London: Nash, 1908. Novel (historical romance; third of the "Katherine Howard" trilogy).

Mr. Apollo. London: Methuen, 1908. Novel.

The "Half Moon." London: Nash, 1909. Novel (historical romance).

A Call. London: Chatto and Windus, 1910. Novel.

Songs from London. London: Elkin Mathews, 1910. Poems.

The Portrait. London: Methuen, 1910. Novel (historical romance).

The Simple Life Limited [pseud. "Daniel Chaucer"]. London: John Lane, 1911. Novel (satire).

Ancient Lights. London: Chapman and Hall, 1911. Reminiscences; published in America in 1911 as *Memories and Impressions*.

Ladies Whose Bright Eyes. London: Constable, 1911. Philadelphia: Lippincott, 1935 (revised). Novel (historical fantasy).

The Critical Attitude. London: Constable, 1911. Essays in literary criticism.

High Germany. London: Duckworth, 1912. Poems.

The Panel. London: Constable, 1912. Novel (farce).

The New Humpty-Dumpty [pseud. "Daniel Chaucer"]. London and New York: John Lane, 1912. Novel (satire).

This Monstrous Regiment of Women. London: Women's Freedom League, 1913. Suffragette pamphlet.

Mr. Fleight. London: Howard Latimer, 1913. Novel (satire).

The Desirable Alien. London: Chatto and Windus, 1913. Impressions of Germany, written in collaboration with Violet Hunt.

The Young Lovell. London: Chatto and Windus, 1913. Novel (historical romance).

Ring for Nancy. Indianapolis: Bobbs-Merrill. New York: Grosset and Dunlap, 1913. Novel (farce; adaptation of *The Panel*; published only in America).

Collected Poems. London: Goschen, 1913; Martin Secker, 1916.

Henry James. London: Martin Secker, 1914. New York: Albert and Charles Boni, 1915. Critical essay.

Antwerp. London: Poetry Workshop, 1915. Long poem (pamphlet).

The Good Soldier. London and New York: John Lane, 1915. Novel.

When Blood Is Their Argument. New York and London: Hodder and Stoughton, 1915. War propaganda (anti-Prussian essays).

Between St. Dennis and St. George. London: Hodder and

Stoughton, 1915. War propaganda (pro-French and anti-Prussian essays).

Zeppelin Nights. London: John Lane, 1915. Historical sketches (told Decameron-fashion against the background of World War I), written in collaboration with Violet Hunt.

The Trail of the Barbarians. London: Longmans, Green, 1917. Translation of the war pamphlet *L'Outrage des Barbares* by Pierre Loti.

On Heaven. London: John Lane, 1918. Poems.

A House. The Chapbook, No. 21. London: Poetry Bookshop, 1921. Long poem (pamphlet).

Thus to Revisit. London: Chapman and Hall, New York: Dutton, 1921. Literary criticism and reminiscence.

The Marsden Case. London: Duckworth, 1923. Novel.

Women and Men. Paris: Three Mountains Press, 1923. Essays.

Mister Bosphorus and the Muses. London: Duckworth, 1923. Long narrative and dramatic poem.

Some Do Not . . . . London: Duckworth. New York: Albert and Charles Boni, 1924. Novel (first of the "Tietjens" tetralogy).

The Nature of a Crime. London: Duckworth. New York: Doubleday, 1924. Novella, written in collaboration with Joseph Conrad; previously published in 1909 in *English Review*.

Joseph Conrad: A Personal Remembrance. London: Duckworth, 1924. Biography, reminiscence, and criticism.

No More Parades. London: Duckworth. New York: Albert and Charles Boni, 1925. Novel (second of the "Tietjens" tetralogy).

A Mirror to France. London: Duckworth, 1926. Sociological impressionism.

A Man Could Stand Up—. London: Duckworth. New York: Albert and Charles Boni, 1926. Novel (third of the "Tietjens" tetralogy).

New Poems. New York: Rudge, 1927.

New York Is Not America. London: Duckworth. New York: Albert and Charles Boni, 1927. Essays in sociological atmospheres.

New York Essays. New York: Rudge, 1927.

The Last Post. London: Duckworth. New York: Literary Guild of America, 1928. Novel (last novel of the "Tietjens" tetralogy; titled *Last Post* in England).

A Little Less Than Gods. New York: Viking Press, 1928. Novel (historical romance).

The English Novel. Philadelphia and London: J. B. Lippincott, 1929. London: Constable, 1930. Essay in literary criticism and history.

No Enemy. New York: Macaulay, 1929. Disguised autobiography (concerning the war years; written shortly after the war).

Return to Yesterday. London: Gollancz, 1931. New York: Horace Liveright, 1932. Reminiscences (up to 1914).

When the Wicked Man. New York: Horace Liveright, 1931. Novel.

The Rash Act. New York: Long and Smith, London: Jonathan Cape, 1933. Novel.

It Was the Nightingale. Philadelphia and London: J. B. Lippincott, 1934. Autobiography and reminiscences (from 1918).

Henry for Hugh. Philadelphia and London: J. B. Lippincott, 1934. Novel.

Provence. Philadelphia and London: J. B. Lippincott, 1935. London: Allen and Unwin, 1938. Impressions of France and England.

Vive le Roy. Philadelphia and London: J. B. Lippincott, 1936. "Mystery" novel.

Collected Poems. New York: Oxford University Press, 1936.

Great Trade Route. New York: Oxford University Press, 1937. London: Allen and Unwin. Impressions of France, the United States, and England.

Portraits from Life. Boston: Houghton Mifflin, 1937. Essays in personal reminiscence and literary criticism about ten *prosateurs* and one poet; published in England in 1938 as *Mightier than the Sword.* London: Allen and Unwin.

The March of Literature. New York: Dial Press, 1938. London: Allen and Unwin, 1939. Survey of literature "From Confucius to Modern Times."

Parade's End. Posthumous publication in America of the "Tietjens" tetralogy in one volume. New York: Alfred A. Knopf, 1950.

The Bodley Head Ford Madox Ford. London: The Bodley Head, 1962–1963. (Four-volume republication of *The Good Soldier*, selected reminiscences and poems, *The Fifth Queen* trilogy, and *Parade's End* without *Last Post*). Introduction by Graham Greene.

Critical Writings of Ford Madox Ford. Edited by Frank Macshane. Regents Critics Series. Lincoln: University of Nebraska Press, 1964.

Letters of Ford Madox Ford. Edited by Richard M. Ludwig. Princeton: Princeton University Press, 1965.

Buckshee. With introductions by Robert Lowell and Kenneth Rexroth. Cambridge, Mass.: Pym-Randall Press, 1966.

Your Mirror to My Times: The Selected Autobiographies and Impressions of Ford Madox Ford. Edited by Michael Killigrew. New York, Chicago, San Francisco: Holt, Rinehart and Winston, 1971.

2. BIOGRAPHICAL AND CRITICAL WRITING ABOUT FORD

Aldington, Richard. *Life for Life's Sake: A Book of Reminiscences.* New York: Viking, 1941.

Andreach, Robert J. *The Slain and Resurrected God: Conrad, Ford, and the Christian Myth.* New York: New York University Press, 1970.

Bowen, Stella. *Drawn from Life.* London: Collins, 1941.

Cassell, Richard A. *Ford Madox Ford: A Study of His Novels.* Baltimore: Johns Hopkins University Press, 1961.

Goldring, Douglas. *The Last Pre-Raphaelite.* London: Macdonald, 1948. Published as *Trained for Genius* in New York: Dutton, 1949.

——. *South Lodge: Reminiscences of Violet Hunt, Ford Madox Ford and the English Review Circle.* London: Constable, 1943.

Gordon, Ambrose, Jr. *The Invisible Tent: The War Novels*

of *Ford Madox Ford.* Austin, Texas: University of Texas Press, 1964.

Gordon, Caroline. *A Good Soldier: A Key to the Novels of Ford Madox Ford.* University of California Library, Davis: Chapbook No. 1, 1963.

Hoffman, Charles G. *Ford Madox Ford.* New York: Twayne Publishers, Inc., 1967.

Hunt, Violet. *The Flurried Years.* London: Hurst and Blackett, 1926. Published as *I Have This to Say.* New York: Boni and Liveright, 1926.

Hynes, Samuel. *Edwardian Occasions: Essays on English Writing in the Early Twentieth Century.* New York: Oxford University Press, 1972.

Jepson, Edgar. *Memories of a Victorian.* London: Gollancz, 1933.

Kenner, Hugh. *Gnomon: Essays on Contemporary Literature.* New York: McDowell, Obolensky, 1958.

——. *The Poetry of Ezra Pound.* London: Faber and Faber, 1951.

——. *The Pound Era.* Berkeley and Los Angeles: University of California Press, 1971.

Leer, Norman. *The Limited Hero in the Novels of Ford Madox Ford.* East Lansing, Michigan State University Press, 1966.

Lid, Richard W. *Ford Madox Ford: The Essence of His Art.* Berkeley and Los Angeles: University of California Press, 1964.

Macauley, Robie. "The Good Ford," *Kenyon Review,* XI (Spring, 1949) , 269–288.

——. Introduction to *Parade's End.* New York: Knopf, 1950.

Macshane, Frank. *Ford Madox Ford: The Critical Heritage.* London and Boston: Routledge and Kegan Paul, 1972.

——. *The Life and Work of Ford Madox Ford.* New York: Horizon Press, 1965.

Meixner, John A. *Ford Madox Ford's Novels: A Critical Study.* Minneapolis, University of Minnesota Press, 1961.

Mizener, Arthur. *The Saddest Story: A Biography of Ford Madox Ford.* New York: World, 1971.

Modern Fiction Studies, IX (Spring, 1963). Issue devoted to Ford.

New Directions: Number Seven. Norfolk, Conn.: New Directions, 1942. Contains "Homage to Ford Madox Ford —a Symposium."

Ohmann, Carol. *Ford Madox Ford: From Apprentice to Craftsman*. Middletown, Conn.: Wesleyan University Press, 1964.

Poli, Bernard J. *Ford Madox Ford and the Transatlantic Review*. Syracuse, New York: Syracuse University Press, 1967.

Pound, Ezra. *Letters: 1907–1941*. Edited by D. D. Paige. New York: Harcourt Brace, 1950.

———. *Pavannes and Divisions*. New York: Knopf, 1918.

———. *Personae*. Norfolk, Conn.: New Directions, 1949.

———. *Polite Essays*. Norfolk, Conn.: New Directions, 1937.

Putnam, Samuel. *Paris Was Our Mistress*. New York: Viking, 1947.

Sewanee Review, LXXIV, Number 4 (Autumn, 1966). Ford Madox Ford: Essays by Caroline Gordon, Neville Braybooke, and Thomas Hanzo.

Smith, Grover. *Ford Madox Ford* in *Six Modern British Novelists*, ed. George Stade. New York and London: Columbia University Press, 1974.

Soskice, Juliet. *Chapters from Childhood*. London: Selwyn and Blount, 1921.

Wells, H. G. *Experiment in Autobiography*. New York: The Macmillan Company, 1934.

Wiley, Paul L. *Novelist of Three Worlds: Ford Madox Ford*. Syracuse, New York: Syracuse University Press, 1962.

Williams, William Carlos. *The Autobiography of William Carlos Williams*. New York: Random House, 1951.

———. *Selected Essays*. New York: Random House, 1954.

———. *Selected Letters*. New York: McDowell, Obolensky, 1957.

Young, Kenneth. *Ford Madox Ford*. Published for The British Council and the National Book League. London, New York, Toronto: Longmans, Green and Co., 1956.

Index

MODERN LITERATURE MONOGRAPHS

In the same series (continued from page ii)